A Gospel Music Life

A Gospel Music Life

An autobiography by
BILLY BLACKWOOD

XULON PRESS

Xulon Press
2301 Lucien Way #415
Maitland, FL 32751
407.339.4217
www.xulonpress.com

© 2020 by Billy Blackwood

All rights reserved solely by the author. The author guarantees all contents are original and do not infringe upon the legal rights of any other person or work. No part of this book may be reproduced in any form without the permission of the author. The views expressed in this book are not necessarily those of the publisher.

Unless otherwise indicated, Scripture quotations taken from the New King James Version (NKJV). Copyright © 1982 by Thomas Nelson, Inc. Used by permission. All rights reserved.

Printed in the United States of America.

ISBN-13: 978-1-6312-9135-7

Endorsements

You cannot write the history of Bill Gaither without including a chapter on the Blackwood Brothers. Bill Lyles, Bill Shaw, R. W. & James Blackwood with Jackie Marshall were at the center of my early musical development. James was one of the very best in our field and his son, Billy, is now carrying on the tradition. I love Billy's heart and urgency in making sure the next generation understands the history and perseverance of this grand group. For all gospel quartet music lovers, this is a must read.

Bill Gaither
Gospel music artist, songwriter and historian
Alexandria, Indiana

I have always looked at the Blackwood Brothers as the "Class" of gospel music. They have always been leaders and icons in the gospel music industry. I am so pleased that Billy is carrying on the tradition of the Blackwood Brothers. While preserving that tradition, Billy has added some of his musical ideas and arrangements that has given it a fresh sound. I am humbled to be asked to write a few words in support of my friend, Billy Blackwood.

Duane Allen
The Oak Ridge Boys
Hendersonville, Tennessee

From childhood I loved to sing. My earliest role model was from The Blackwood Brothers On Tour Live album. James Blackwood was my concept of the perfect voice and presentation. Thus my singing development began. Into my fabric was woven James Blackwood. A piece of that fabric has now opened as a window through which I can peek to see, from the inside, the Blackwood culture that helped form me. It has reinforced what I hoped it would be.

Billy Blackwood has written a book. Unknowingly, he has written it just for me. The highs, the lows, the challenges, the victories, the polished, the unpolished and the raw material are all there. It paints an excellent picture. It is a testimony of God and His amazing provision. It paints a picture of a hero and the results of faithful service to the King.

I cannot recommend this book too highly. It simply states that God can move through the celebrity and the agony of life. The end result is a diamond in the crown of Jesus.

Rev. Dr. Howard S. Russell
Former President & CEO
Christian Healthcare Ministries
Barberton, Ohio

Billy Blackwood is not only a gifted musician who sings the gospel but he lives it. His must-read life heritage and story in gospel music is candidly transparent yet masterfully seasoned with God's amazing grace. Billy's redemptive journey is a real life-changer, from emptiness, brokenness and repentance, to faith, transformation and restoration.

Buddy Smith
Senior Vice President, American Family Association
Tupelo, Mississippi

GROWING UP ON an Alabama farm in the 1940's, our family's entertainment consisted almost exclusively of the radio (for millennials, that was a box with a battery out of which came speaking and singing, etc.). My family were Gospel quartet fans, and The Blackwood Brothers topped the list. We first saw them in person in 1951. From that time, I have never missed an opportunity to see and hear them, and, even today few days pass that I don't listen to them. My Gospel quartet recordings include some 17,000 songs, including every song recorded by The Blackwood Brothers and radio programs not sold to the general public. To become personal friends with them (at least six have spent the night in our home and others have visited) was something I could never have imagined as a lad. The Blackwood name is enshrined with other names such as Vaughn, Stamps, Speer and LeFevre. Billy kindly allowed me to preview several chapters in the book. It is a must for Blackwood fans in particular and for Gospel music fans in general, because it brings to the fore family stories which are not widely known.

The Hon. L. E. (Ed) Gosa
Former Judge for Lamar County, Alabama
Vernon, Alabama

Daddy and me, circa 1955

Dedication

I want to dedicate this book to the memory of my sweet daddy,
James Blackwood, Sr.,
whose pioneering spirit and can-do attitude
paved the way for our family and ministry.

Acknowledgements

I wish to thank those who read portions of this manuscript and offered their advice and encouragement; Bill Gaither, Duane Allen, Rev. Dr. Howard Russell, Buddy Smith, The Hon. Ed Gosa, Ed Leonard, Danny Jones, Jim Black, and Dr. Bob Orr.

I also wish to thank my precious wife, Cherry, who did the same, and who reminds me every time I think of her how gracious, merciful and extravagant God's love is for me.

I wish to thank my music industry heroes and fellow travelers, many of whom are mentioned in this book, whose journeys have intersected mine and made my life better for it.

Most of all, I wish to thank God for loving me, forgiving me, restoring me, and allowing me the privilege of knowing Him and serving Him with the gifts He has given me. All glory to Him.

Preface

EACH OF US HAS A STORY; A STORY THAT IS uniquely our own, a chronicle of our journey through life as we know it and have experienced it. This is my story.

Growing up in a gospel music family in the middle of the twentieth century has afforded me an unusual journey, and due to the timing of my birth I have been privileged to meet people and experience situations that have become part of my story.

It is my hope that as you read my story you will find places where your story intersects mine and that in doing so you will find that we are connected perhaps more than it would appear at first glance.

As our stories connect and our pieces of the puzzle find their place in the big picture of life it is my prayer that my journey and your journey will lead us to the same conclusions, and that we will find ourselves a part of something far greater than we would have found apart.

Billy Blackwood

TABLE OF CONTENTS

1. Humble Beginnings 1
2. The 1930s & '40s–From Choctaw To Shenandoah 7
3. Moving To Memphis 18
4. The Crash 28
5. A New Blackwood Brothers 36
6. The Statesmen Quartet 45
7. The Blackwood 'Little' Brothers 51
8. J. D. Sumner 55
9. Gospel Drums 63
10. Elvis and the Blackwood Brothers 77
11. Elvis and Voice 87
12. Rededication 97
13. Gordon Jensen and Sunrise 103
14. Andrus, Blackwood & Co. 108
15. The U.S. and Abroad 114
16. The Hendersonville Chapel 122
17. Fathers Day 126
18. Daddy & Mama 131
19. No-Mader What 141
20. Gateway 145
21. Divorce 150
22. Restoration 155
23. Past To Present 162

Epilogue 177
Appendix One 181
About the Author 183

Prologue

I WAS UP TO MY ELBOWS AND EYEBALLS IN A messy mix of diesel fuel and oil spraying out of the back of the bus, as were several other members of the Stamps Quartet; my brother, Jimmy, Donnie Sumner, Mylon LeFevre, Tony Brown and Jimmy 'Duke' Dumas. J. D. was behind the steering wheel, and Jim Hill was..., well, let's just say there was no more room behind the bus.

The reason the engine wouldn't crank escapes me all these years later and, although it seems like we had pushed the old 35' Flexible bus over half of downtown Ft. Worth, the truth was probably closer to two blocks. The six of us were lined up across the back of the bus trying to push it far and fast enough to get it to crank, the theory being that if it could gain enough momentum, J. D. could 'pop' the clutch, throw it into gear, and the engine just might start.

Best I recall we were finally successful, but what I am sure of is that they never taught that in "How To Be In A Full-time Gospel Quartet." And to think, it was the Blackwood Brothers who first introduced the concept of using a customized bus to meet the transportation needs of a musical group!

1

Humble Beginnings

Sharecroppers were a part of the American farming landscape for decades, particularly in the South in the midst of the Great Depression of the 1930s. For those unfamiliar with the term, a sharecropper lived on land they didn't own, in a house (usually a roughly nailed together shack) they also didn't own, farming for the person who owned the land and the shack and the farm. The payment for their work was a share of the crop they harvested; hence the name, sharecropper. They worked very hard and, in many cases, barely survived on the share they received. They were so low down on the socio-economic totem pole there wasn't much place to go but up.

The Blackwoods were sharecroppers in Choctaw County, Mississippi, in the heart of the South in the early 1900s. The oldest of ten children, William Emmett, married Carrie Savala Prewitt in 1898. On Christmas Eve, 1900, they had their first child, a son, whom they named Roy Emmett. Next was a daughter, born on New Year's Eve 1903, named Lena Madeline. Then another son was born to them on August 22, 1911, whom they named Doyle Jimmie. Last, but not least, was a son, born on August 4th, 1919, named James Webre.

Emmett and Carrie often worked side by side in the fields, and Carrie tended the home and the children as they came along. Carrie also became the unofficial midwife of the area and, in her lifetime of serving as such, assisted in the delivery of ninety-nine babies!

As the Blackwood boys grew, they helped their dad in the field, primarily picking cotton, a common cash crop in the red clay hills of Mississippi. Emmett and the boys would also hunt for supper, hopefully bringing home a squirrel or a rabbit for Carrie to prepare for the family's evening meal. Life was hard and amusement was practically non-existent. At Christmas, the kids would get an apple or an orange, and a nickel. If it had been a productive year, they might also get a bag of hard candy, a shirt or overalls.

I remember a story my dad told of praying for a little red wagon for Christmas. I think he was about seven years old at the time. On Christmas morning, Santa had brought the bag of hard candy, a shirt and overalls, but no red wagon. Later that day, they went to have Christmas dinner with a rich uncle in Louisville, Mississippi. Under the tree at his house were bicycles, trains, toys and games, and a little red wagon. My dad was heartbroken it was for someone other than him.

Several months later, my grandmother wakened him for school and, as he entered the front room, there sat a shiny red wagon! My dad thought Santa had finally come through. Later that day his older brother, Doyle, spilled the truth when he shared that my grandmother had been saving her egg money for months to get the little red wagon my dad so deeply wanted. Times were hard but love was strong.

The shacks the family lived in would usually consist of three, or at best, four rooms; a living space, a kitchen, and one or two bedrooms (well, there was one other room, but it was usually not attached to the house). Moving from shack to shack and farm to farm was a common occurrence. You went where the work was.

I remember hearing a comedian talk about growing up in such an environment, describing how hard times were, having no running water, no heat except the fireplace in the winter, and no air conditioning except to open the doors in the summer and hope there was a breeze, and barely enough food to survive. He'd add, "And then came the Depression!"

Those were humble beginnings for sure. But one thing the Blackwood family had that sustained them through those times was their faith in God. They attended an old country church, at least a mile or more from wherever they happened to be living and farming at the time. Going to church on Sunday was the big event of any and every week. They would load up the wagon if they had one at the time, or walk if they had to, but they were going to church. Attendance was non-negotiable. Rising early to make the trip, gathering to sing the hymns of the church, listening to the preacher bring a message from the Bible, enjoying the fellowship of neighbors, and then making the trip back home usually filled most of the daylight hours on Sundays.

On special occasions they would have all day singing and dinner on the grounds. That's pretty self-explanatory but, to the uninitiated, families would gather out under the towering trees after church, spread blankets and meals they had prepared, and eat as one after another solo, duet, trio or quartet sang a familiar song from the hymn book. It was like a picnic with a spiritual emphasis.

In 1918, my grandmother Blackwood, a morally good, churchgoing woman, attended a revival meeting in which she became aware of her need for a true salvation experience, something more than just living right and going to church; a real relationship with Jesus, Who would live inside her and fill her with His Spirit. She was the first person to the altar and became a different person that night, and something happened there that completely changed the

Blackwood family and laid the foundation for the music ministry that would become the Blackwood Brothers Quartet.

As I recall hearing my dad tell the story passed down to him, she would take her Bible and go out to a stump far enough away from the house where she could pray aloud without thought of who might hear her. She would kneel at that stump and open her Bible, lay it on the stump and read and pray, and read and pray some more. She began to pray for the members of her family to come to this realization of a personal relationship with Jesus, and one by one, they did! My dad, James, was born in the summer of 1919 as this wave of revival and spiritual awakening impacted the Blackwood family. At just six years old he gave his heart to Christ in that old country church.

One of grandma's prayers was for her oldest son, Roy. Roy had moved away from Mississippi and was working in a store when his mother's prayers began to produce a conviction in his heart that he needed to know God personally and move back home to the family in Ackerman. Moving back to Mississippi, he too, surrendered his heart and life to Christ and soon afterward felt the call to become a minister. During this time, Roy and his wife, Susie, had their first child, a son, named R.W. Interestingly, neither the R. nor the W. stood for anything. His name was simply R.W.

Spiritual revival was taking place in this rural, middle-of-nowhere farming community, and the Blackwood boys came of age as it swept through the area. In those years, life consisted of working in the fields and attending revivals and church meetings, as members of both my grandparents' families came to know Christ. It was in this rural setting that the Blackwood Brothers Quartet was born.

First picture of the Blackwood Brothers Quartet, l-r, R.W., James, Roy, Doyle

First professional picture of the group, l-r, Roy, James, R.W., Doyle

Mr. & Mrs. William Emmett Blackwood, parents of the Blackwood Brothers

The 1930s & '40s–From Choctaw To Shenandoah

DADDY AND MY UNCLE DOYLE SANG DUETS together all over Choctaw County, Mississippi. They also attended singing schools, most notably one taught by Vardaman Ray, who was a well-respected singer in that area. At the end of one of his ten-day singing schools, he asked my dad and Doyle if they would like to join him in a new quartet. Gene Catledge would join them on bass, and their first concert was at Concord Baptist Church, just south of Ackerman, the county seat. As they were about to begin someone asked them the name of their group. They didn't have one, and someone quickly suggested the name, Choctaw County Jubilee Singers. They sang together for about a year, but that was enough to open the Blackwood boys' eyes and hearts to the possibility of singing together professionally.

By the early 1930s Doyle was in his early twenties and James was entering his teens. Roy had moved to North Carolina, where he was pastoring. Doyle had moved to Birmingham and was singing with the Homeland Harmony Quartet, but in 1934 they moved back to Choctaw County and soon began to pursue the idea of singing together as a family. As Roy, Doyle, James and R.W. sang, people began to notice and remark at how well they sounded singing together. There is often a musical dynamic that happens when families sing together. The blend of the timbre of their collective voices achieves a sound that is unlike non-familial voices (note the Carter Family, the Gatlin Brothers and the Mandrell Sisters of country music fame, the Ames Brothers, Williams Brothers, the Lennon Sisters, the Pointer Sisters, the Osmond Brothers, and the Jackson Five of pop music).

The Blackwood Brothers began singing together in local churches and the word began to spread. They showed up at a radio station not far from home, WHEF, in Kosciusko, Mississippi, and asked the station manager if they could sing on the air. Radio was live during those years and once the guys began to sing, the phone began to ring with people calling in to request hearing them sing a particular hymn. While the manager initially agreed to allow them fifteen minutes on the air, the phone calls and their vast repertoire of songs had them on the air for an hour and fifteen minutes, which was five times the original allotted time. The manager was thrilled to have quality live music, and the Blackwood Brothers were happy to oblige. He offered them a weekly radio program on the spot.

As their popularity grew, opportunity grew with it. The brothers set their sights on the capital city of Jackson, Mississippi and WJDX Radio. WHEF in Kosciusko was a 250-watt station and barely reached out of Attala County. They auditioned for WJDX, a 5,000-watt station in Jackson and were awarded with a daily radio program. The year was 1937. With this move their audience jumped exponentially and invitations to have the guys sing began to pour in from all over the southern part of Mississippi.

One such invitation was to a small Baptist church in the little town of Weathersby, about thirty miles south of Jackson, Mississippi. As they sang that day, James noticed a beautiful young lady, whose name he would soon learn was Miriam Grantham. Miriam's father was the local postman and, although the Depression was still making for tough times in many parts of the country, having a government job meant that the Granthams were one of the more well-to-do families in the little community. Miriam had heard the boys on the radio station from Jackson and had even called in a request on occasion.

Depending on who is telling the story, James, after the concert was over, made his way to find Miriam, or Miriam positioned herself to be found. Miriam had strategically written her name on a songbook she was carrying in her arms, which could be easily read by anyone wanting to notice. James wanted to notice, and he not only saw the name but recognized it as the name of someone who had called the radio station to make a request. It made for instant conversation (she says he took the bait). Miriam mentioned her mother had offered to have the boys over for pie and coffee after the service that morning, to which James readily agreed. That encounter led to a courtship and a marriage. Doyle had also struck up a relationship with a young lady named Lavez Hawkins. They, too, planned to be married. The two couples celebrated a double wedding ceremony on May 4th, 1939.

Gospel music was beginning to make great inroads into the culture of southern life. James D. Vaughn, often mentioned as the father of four-part male quartet music, began to publish songbooks for the growing number of groups singing gospel quartet music. V.O. and Frank Stamps began to do the same from their base in Dallas, Texas. J.R. Baxter soon partnered with V.O. Stamps to form the Stamps-Baxter Music Publishing Company, which is still in existence today. In fact, these publishers began to look for groups to put under contract to sing only from their songbooks and sell the books in their concerts to produce revenue for the publishing companies and gospel music as a money-making industry was born!

In late 1939, the Blackwood Brothers had the opportunity to make another move, this time to Shreveport, Louisiana. KWKH was a 10,000-watt radio station that made the leap to 50,000 watts shortly after the group arrived. The Blackwood Brothers sang on the air twice a day, at 6:30 a.m. and 12:30 p.m. With this powerful radio station behind them, their music was being heard across much of the southern mid-section of the USA, and in these days before the advent of television, practically everyone listened to radio on a daily basis. This move greatly expanded their musical outreach and their concert schedule. It was about this time that the Blackwood Brothers signed a contract with the Stamps-Baxter Company and, to aid in their concert appearances, the Stamps-Baxter Company sent a young pianist named Joe Roper to accompany the group.

As this gospel quartet and songbook industry began to thrive, the Blackwood Brothers observed that the South was becoming overrun with gospel quartets traveling the roads selling songbooks. So, in 1940, with the endorsement and support of the Stamps-Baxter organization, they made yet another move, which turned out to be strategic in God's plan for the group and their families. They relocated to the North; Iowa, in fact; Shenandoah, Iowa, to be exact. Most have never heard of this little town in the Southwest corner of the state of Iowa. The population was about 5,000 at the time, peaking at almost 7,000 in 1950. Once referred to as the "seed and nursery center of the world," Shenandoah is the home to Earl May Seed Company and the radio station KMA, founded by Mr. May. Although KMA was not a clear channel station, the open topography of the plains allowed their coverage to reach a huge swath of the Plains states and into southern Canada as well. The early live radio stations gave many performers their start. Initially they were known as the Blackwood Brothers Stamps-Baxter Quartet.

When the Blackwood Brothers became a part of the KMA family, it is estimated that over a million people a day heard their live radio programs broadcasting from that little town with the big radio station! My dad once told me they regularly received mail from as far away as Manitoba in southern Canada and northern Texas. One of the regular performers was Ike Everly, a favorite of the folks who loved country music. Ike's sons, Don and Phil, aka, The Everly Brothers, made their debut there, standing on chairs to reach the microphones.

The Blackwood Brothers had no sooner established their homes and lives in Shenandoah than Japan bombed Pearl Harbor and plunged the United States into World War II. The families moved to San Diego, California shortly thereafter, continuing to sing and keep a group together, even though R.W. was drafted into the military and served in the Pacific. He was in the Philippines victory celebration on Christmas Day 1944 and shipped to Okinawa in April 1945. James worked in Rohrer Aircraft Plant as a welder helping with the war effort. It was in San Diego that R.W., Jr., and James, Jr. (Jimmy) were born. During the war, Doyle was not drafted and, after a short time in California, moved back to the South, to Chattanooga, Tennessee, where he worked as a deejay at a gospel radio station. While he lived there, he met Bill Lyles, and immediately recognized his great talent as a bass singer. He and his wife, Lavez, also had their first child, Richard Terrell (Terry), who would go on to sing with the Imperials many years later.

There were many key personnel in the Blackwood Brothers during the years in Iowa and in California during the war. In particular were Hilton Griswold, originally from Cameron, Texas, who served as the group's pianist throughout the '40s, Don Smith, a great bass singer from one of the Stamps Quartets in Texas who had moved to work in the aircraft plants during the war, Troy Chafin, who took over as tenor in San Diego, A.T. and Lavera Humphries, A.T. singing and Lavera playing piano, Bill Lyles on bass, and Calvin

Newton and Cat Freeman on tenor. Cat was a brother to another famous gospel music personality, Vestal Goodman!

After the war ended the Blackwoods returned to Iowa, and once again made Shenandoah their base, singing daily on the radio and traveling to every town within driving distance for concert appearances. The decision was made at this time to sever their relationship with the Stamps organization and once again they were simply The Blackwood Brothers Quartet. Don Smith moved to Iowa with the group but then returned to California in 1947, landing in Fresno. Shortly after, Doyle rejoined the family there. Doyle convinced Bill Lyles to move with him to Iowa to sing bass for the group. Their popularity grew to the point that they formed a second quartet in 1948! James and R.W. led the Blackwood Brothers, and Roy and Doyle led the new second group, called the Blackwood Gospel Quartet. The North had officially adopted these boys from Mississippi and welcomed them into their homes and their hearts. To this day, whenever we appear in that part of the country (Iowa, Missouri, Nebraska, Kansas, South Dakota), people still tell us stories of when they were little kids and heard the Blackwood Brothers, or how their mom and dad had the group in their home to eat, which was a common occurrence in those days.

They remained in Shenandoah until 1950 when they once again made a decision to move, this time back to the South, which affected not only their careers but, as you'll read in the next chapter, the careers of other up-and-coming musical artists as well.

James Blackwood walking on Capitol Street in Jackson, MS, circa 1938

Miriam Blackwood's High School graduation picture, 1939.
Mama was the valedictorian of her senior class.

James & Miriam's wedding day, May 4, 1939

The BBQ at KMA Radio in Shenandoah, Iowa, circa 1946, l-r, Roy, James, R.W., Don Smith, seated, Hilton Griswold

The BBQ at KMA Radio in Shenandoah, Iowa, circa 1947, l-r, Calvin Newton, James, R.W., Bill Lyles, seated, Hilton Griswold

The BBQ and families at KMA Radio in Shenandoah, Iowa, circa 1947, adults l-r, James & Miriam Blackwood, Elaine & R. W. Blackwood, seated, Hilton Griswold, standing, Marie Griswold, Bill & Ruth Lyles, Lavez & Doyle Blackwood, Susie, Cecil & Roy Blackwood. Children, l-r, Jimmy, Ron, R.W., Jr., Barbara Griswold, Larry Griswold (in Hilton's lap), Billy & Gary Lyles, Terry & Kaye Blackwood.

The BBQ in Iowa before the days of busses, circa 1948, l-r, R.W., James, Doyle, Bill Lyles, Hilton Griswold, Roy.

The BBQ at in Shenandoah, circa 1949, l-r, R.W., Alden Toney, James, Bill Lyles, Squatting, Hilton Griswold

James Blackwood, circa 1950

Moving To Memphis

While still in Shenandoah in the late '40s, older brothers Roy and Doyle began to realize that traveling was taking a physical toll on them. Roy was approaching fifty, Doyle nearing forty, while James and R.W. were just thirty and twenty-eight, respectively. The younger two had seemingly boundless energy and loved the travel and the concerts; not so true for Roy and Doyle. At the same time, their parents (Emmett and Carrie) were aging in Mississippi. Farm life had been a hard life and the years of hard work were quickly catching up with them.

So, the family decided to say goodbye to their adopted life in Shenandoah and move back to the South to be available for their parents. Moving back to the rural roads of north-central Mississippi would not have been conducive to travel, so the decision was made to choose Memphis, Tennessee as home base. Memphis occupies the southwest corner of the state of Tennessee and borders Mississippi to the south and Arkansas to the west. Locating there allowed them close proximity to their parents while at the same time gave them a major city from which to continue their career as musical artists and even increase their fan-base from this "Hub of the Mid-South."

Memphis, in 1950, was a city of 400,000 people. Having grown up on a farm in the hills of Mississippi, then relocating to a Midwest farm town of 4-5,000 in the '40s, moving to Memphis was definitely a jump to the big city. Memphis was the hub of the Mid-South as far as being the distribution center of the vast cotton producing farms of West Tennessee, Eastern Arkansas and Northern Mississippi. Memphis had also established itself as a center of Blues music, second only to New Orleans. W.C. Handy was a well-known blues musician of his day and Beale Street became known as a place where patrons could come to hear this truly American art form played at its best.

Roy and Doyle had decided to retire from traveling by the time of the move to Memphis and very shortly afterwards began to operate a retail music outlet in downtown Memphis at 186 Jefferson Street, fittingly named The Blackwood Brothers Record Shop. The store was a joint venture between all the brothers, but was primarily operated by Roy and Doyle, while James and R.W. continued as the core of the Blackwood Brothers Quartet. It would later relocate to 209 N. Lauderdale, and many hundreds of gospel music fans would stop and shop there over the years.

As already noted, there were many key personnel in the Blackwood Brothers during the early years. The tenor spot, in particular, hosted some of the greatest tenors ever to sing a gospel song, including Calvin Newton in 1948, Cat Freeman in 1949, Aldon Toney in 1950-51, and Dan Huskey in 1951-52. These were all phenomenal singers and added richly to the voices of James and R.W. and Bill Lyles. In 1952, one of the greatest of the greats, Bill Shaw, joined the Blackwood Brothers at the tenor spot. Bill was the perfect complement to the Blackwood Brothers sound. While the tenors before him were good, they each lasted a short time. Bill, however, sang first tenor with the Blackwood Brothers for twenty-one years!

The move to Memphis also brought about another big change for the group. Hilton Griswold, who had played piano and sung with the group for the entire decade of the '40s decided to go into full-time ministry in Iowa. He would not be making the move to Memphis. In his place, my dad hired a young man from Jacksonville, Florida named Jackie Marshall. While losing Hilton seemed to be a step backwards, God had other ideas. Jackie wowed audiences and literally took the group to another level, both musically and professionally.

In 1951, the Blackwood Brothers signed a recording contract with RCA Victor records, meaning that their records were now distributed around the world. The great gospel music songwriter, recording artist and historian, Bill Gaither, has stated that this group consisting of James, R.W., Bill Lyles, Bill Shaw, and Jack Marshall on piano was the greatest gospel quartet ever. Their stage charisma was infectious and their singing was second to none.

It was into this era of the Blackwood Brothers that I made my debut; not with the group, but into the world. On April 7, 1953 I was born at Baptist Hospital in Memphis.

Once they made the move to Memphis they also made the decision to buy a private plane to enable them to travel greater distances from home in much shorter time than driving. At the same time, their popularity reached the point where they began to make monthly concert appearances at Ellis Auditorium, the city's downtown concert venue.

One young fan who attended many of those concerts was Elvis Presley. The Presleys had moved to Memphis in 1948 and began attending First Assembly of God Church, also the home church of the Blackwoods upon their arrival in 1950. In fact, the quartet would often sing a song in the services there at First Assembly and it is likely that Elvis first heard the group at church. The Presleys lived in Lauderdale Courts, a low-income housing project just blocks from the Ellis Auditorium, and when the downtown concerts started occurring regularly, he also attended as many of those as his meager income would allow.

There is a story from those days that the young Elvis stood outside the ticket window of the Ellis Auditorium for one of the concerts but didn't have the money to buy a ticket. My dad saw him and recognized him as a young man who frequented the concerts and, having some idea of his financial limitations, gave him a ticket for the concert. The story continues that not long after that concert, Elvis came to a concert with the money for a ticket and, once inside, saw my dad, who wrote him a check from the concert account to reimburse him for his ticket and told him his ticket would be complimentary from now on. While I was not around to witness those events and, with the understanding that I may not be accurate with all the details, one thing I did see many years later was the check written from my dad to Elvis framed and hanging in a display case in the wardrobe and memorabilia room at Graceland, which validated at least part of the story.

The up-and-coming artists of that era influenced by the Blackwood Brothers is quite a list. The first concert Harold and Don Reid ever attended was a Blackwood Brothers concert near their hometown of Staunton, Virginia. That night those two brothers decided that singing in a quartet was their dream. They asked their friends, Phil Balsley and Lew DeWitt to join them, and the Statler Brothers were born, first singing together in 1955. On their 1974 record album *Thank You, World*, they recorded a song telling how the Blackwood Brothers influenced them. The song is aptly titled, "The Blackwood Brothers By The Statler Brothers."

In 1964, the Statler Brothers became the backup group for another Blackwood Brothers fan. There was a poor farming family that lived in Dyess, Arkansas, working in the cotton fields. They would come in for lunch every day and listen to the Blackwood

Brothers over WMPS Radio from Memphis. The son of this family came to Memphis seeking a career in music, which proved to be overwhelmingly successful. Johnny Cash later wrote a gospel song called "Over the Next Hill We'll Be Home," which the Blackwood Brothers recorded. A copy of the letter Johnny wrote to my dad after hearing their recording appears at the end of this chapter.

I recall my dad telling the story of meeting Tammy Wynette at a Grammy Awards ceremony in Nashville. She had just been awarded the top female vocalist award in country music. My dad walked up to her and said, "Tammy, I'm James Blackwood, and I want to congratulate you winning the Grammy award this year." She replied, "James, you don't remember me but I remember you. When you used to broadcast live from WMPS at noon in Memphis, some of us girls from the telephone company where I worked would walk over there at lunch to watch and hear you."

Larry Gatlin writes, "My first hero was James Blackwood, of the Blackwood Brothers Quartet. The first time I heard James sing 'I Want to Be More Like Jesus' I just knew somehow from that moment that I wanted to be a singer for the rest of my life." From Larry Gatlin and the Gatlin Brothers to Barbara Mandrell and the Mandrell Sisters, the list goes on.

In the early 1950s the most popular program on television was *Arthur Godfrey's Talent Scouts*, a program dedicated to the discovery of new talent, much like *American Idol*, *The Voice*, *America's Got Talent* and other popular programs in recent history. All of America tuned in to see and hear who would walk away with the honor of winning *Talent Scouts*. Older folks will remember that in the early years of television, there were only three channels from which to choose: ABC, CBS and NBC (I wonder why there was more to watch on TV when there were only three channels than there is now when there are 300! But, I digress).

Though by 1954 the Blackwood Brothers had been singing for twenty years, they were only known in the South and the Midwest when they were invited to be a contestant on Mr. Godfrey's program. Talent Scouts was a secular program and the powers that be stated that their song could not be overtly religious in nature. That evening, June 14, 1954, the Blackwood Brothers sang a rousing number made famous by fellow Memphian Kay Starr called "Have You Talked To The Man Upstairs," which was a direct reference to God without saying so explicitly. The contestants performed and the winner was chosen by means of an applause meter, which registered the volume and intensity of the live audience's applause. When it came time to vote by applauding, the crowd overwhelmingly chose the Blackwood Brothers as the winner with their thunderous ovation. You may hear the actual audio recording of the group's performance on Mr. Godfrey's program by typing this URL into your search bar: http://bit.ly/2VfdBIe. The group's introduction begins at 8:00 minutes.

The night they won *Talent Scouts*, RCA realized they had a hit on their hands and hurriedly arranged for the group to go into RCA studios in New York the next day to record "Have You Talked To The Man Upstairs." It went to the top ten of RCA records. Overnight all of America was now aware of this young gospel quartet from Memphis, Tennessee. The winner of *Talent Scouts* stayed in New York the following week and appeared on Mr. Godfrey's daily radio and television program, simulcast across the country on CBS. On the daily programs the Blackwood Brothers were allowed to sing any material of their choosing and my dad remembered that on one of those daily programs, Mr. Godfrey had tears on his cheeks as they sang, "His Hand in Mine." Though the programs ran the entire week, the Blackwood Brothers begged out of Friday's program due to the fact that their monthly concert in Memphis happened to fall on that day. They flew from New York back to Memphis after

Thursday's show in order to be in Memphis in time for the concert the following evening.

That homecoming in Memphis had the feeling of a World Series champion team parade. The Ellis Auditorium was built with two concert halls facing each other sharing a common stage, separated by a soundproof fire curtain. The curtain was raised that night and both the north and south halls of Ellis Auditorium were filled, and still people were turned away. The Blackwood Brothers were playing to the home crowd and the crowd loved every minute of it. To say they were flying high was an understatement. Every concert was standing room only and overflowing. Unfortunately, the sky was the limit.

The BBQ on stage, l-r, Dan Huskey, James, R.W., Billy Lyles, circa 1951

The BBQ promo picture, top, Jackie Marshall (pianist), 2nd row, Bill Shaw, tenor, Bill Lyles, bass, 3rd row, James and R.W., circa, 1952

Jackie Marshall

SRO crowds were a normal event, circa early 1950s

The Blackwood Brothers and the McGuire Sisters pictured in a CBS studio in New York as they joined together to sing "Lead Me To That Rock," on Godfrey's Morning Program.

The BBQ & The McGuire Sisters on Arthur Godfrey's Talent Scouts, June 14, 1954

The BBQ returning to Memphis after winning Talent Scouts and receiving an honorary day, June 18, 1954

Blackwood Brothers Quartet Day Proclamation, June 18, 1954

4

THE CRASH

NOT LONG AFTER MOVING TO MEMPHIS, THE demands for concert appearances began to grow throughout the South and even beyond. They had always traveled by car, which on the pre-interstate highways of the early 1950s made for some long nights getting back home. Moving to Memphis presented the option of flying in and out of a major hub, which would drastically cut their travel time and allow them more time at home between touring. They purchased their first plane in 1952, a twin Cessna followed later by a Cessna 195. R.W. Blackwood and Bill Lyles both got pilot licenses, and away they went. Both aircraft were pretty tight quarters and it wasn't long before they needed more room and purchased a Beechcraft G18, which seated ten passengers. This gave them ample room for their sound system and merchandise as well.

The Blackwood Brothers were one of, if not the first, to utilize private air travel for a touring music group. While the quartet was residing in and touring from Shenandoah, Iowa in the 1940s, there was a young man from not-too-far-away Clarinda, Iowa, who was making a huge splash in the music world. Glenn Miller had risen to fame and, along with his orchestra, created some of the most memorable American music ever heard. His "Chattanooga Choo-Choo" was the first certified gold record, selling over a million copies.

After enlisting in the army at age thirty-eight, Glenn formed an army band and toured extensively, providing entertainment to troops in England during World War II. He was tragically killed on December 15th, 1944 when the single engine plane in which he was flying from London to Paris disappeared over the English Channel, the first such death of a music celebrity at the height of his career. The music world mourned the loss of one of its greats at a much too young forty years old.

Unfortunately, the same fate awaited the Blackwood Brothers when, not quite ten years later, tragedy would strike. On June 29, 1954, just two weeks after winning *Arthur Godfrey's Talent Scouts*, the quartet sang to a packed high school auditorium in Gulfport, Mississippi, their meteoric rise to celebrity status being felt everywhere they went. The next day they flew their Beechcraft G18 to the little town of Clanton, Alabama for an appearance at the annual Chilton County Peach Festival.

In the early 1950s, the Blackwood Brothers had partnered with Hovie Lister and the Statesmen Quartet to form a team that traveled across much of the South and later across the Southwest and up the West coast to present this unique brand of music. The Statesmen were there in Clanton to appear with the Blackwood Brothers in concert that evening. It was a warm Wednesday afternoon when the crowds began to gather for that evening's performance. The concert was to be held at the local airport, in part because the airplane hangar was the largest facility in town, and a huge crowd was expected. The Blackwood Brothers had flown in earlier that day, while the Statesmen had driven from their home base in Atlanta.

The sound system was set up, the merchandise tables in place, and the members of both quartets mingled with adoring fans, many of which began arriving well before the actual concert time. This was the first time the group had flown into the town of Clanton and, as such, the flight out after the concert would be a first. R.W. and Bill thought it a good idea to practice a takeoff while it was still daylight, to familiarize them with the length of the strip. As they walked to the plane, the son of the chairman of the Peach Festival, Johnny Ogburn, asked if he could join them for the practice trip. That would prove to be a fateful request.

The three climbed into the small twin Beechcraft and proceeded to taxi down the runway while James, Bill Shaw, Jack Marshall, the members of the Statesmen, and fans watched as the aircraft lifted off and made a circle in the nearby airspace before coming in for a landing. As I recall my dad telling this story, upon approach, they touched down once but lifted off to make another loop, possibly thinking they needed a slightly different approach. The second time they attempted touchdown, something went tragically wrong. They bounced once on the runway and the plane lifted again, but this time the flaps were not set correctly and the plane went straight up a couple of hundred feet in the air where it stalled and came plummeting back to earth with a horrendous impact, bursting into flames, which immediately consumed the plane and its occupants.

Panic overtook my dad, who began to run toward the plane in a vain attempt to rescue his beloved nephew, R.W. and his best friend, Bill Lyles. He later recalled that he could see R.W.'s lifeless form in the flames. As he charged toward the plane, someone caught him from behind and held him back from the flames. The others witnessing this tragedy stood in horror as if somehow this was not really happening. Bill Lyles was thirty-four, and R.W. was thirty-two. Johnny Ogburn, the third passenger in the plane, was twenty years old.

Only two weeks before, the Blackwood Brothers had won a nationally televised contest, had been rushed into RCA studios in

New York City the next day to record "Have You Talked to The Man Upstairs," the song they sang to win the contest. Their career had truly taken off and God only knows where things were headed from there. But it all came crashing down that day in Clanton, Alabama.

The Statesmen put James in their car and returned him to Memphis. Since the quartet had just won *Talent Scouts* and had become overnight celebrities, the news of the crash hit the national news feeds. As they tried to wrap their minds around this horrific event, all of America mourned with the families and remaining members of the group. My dad was so grief-stricken he could not function for days. This was a bad dream from which there was no awakening. The family's pastor, James E. Hamill, father of future gospel singer Jim Hamill, had the grievous responsibility of informing R.W. and Bill's wives of the passing of their husbands.

Their combined funeral was held at the Ellis Auditorium, on the same stage where they had sung barely two weeks earlier after flying home from New York. It was the largest funeral in the history of Memphis until Elvis Presley's funeral twenty-three years later. Although there is no proof, it is thought that Elvis was likely in attendance at R.W. and Bill's funeral, and perhaps even his mother and dad. The Speer Family sang "Someone to Care."

The great gospel songwriter, Mosie Lister, wrote a song in honor of R.W. and Bill called "There Are Two New Voices (In The Heavenly Choir)," which the Statesmen recorded. If there were to be a continuance of the Blackwood Brothers Quartet, its history would forever be delineated by the tragedy of the airplane crash, both before and after.

The BBQ's Beechcraft G18, the group's private plane.

R.W. Blackwood & Bill Lyles, pilot and co-pilot, in the cockpit

This was the last picture made of the quartet before the fatal plane crash. This was made in Gulfport, Miss., the night of June 29, 1954.

The BBQ in Gulfport, MS, June 29, 1954, the night before the plane crash

Plane wreckage

Plane wreckage

R.W. & Bill's funeral at the Ellis Auditorium,
Memphis' downtown concert hall

"There Are Two New Voices (In The Heavenly Choir)" sheet music, a song written by Mosie Lister, and recorded by The Statesmen Quartet of Atlanta, GA

Jim "Big Chief" Wetherington, the bass vocalist for the Statesmen Quartet, fills in with the Blackwood Brothers in the months after the plane crash. This is one of the first pictures with Cecil Blackwood, R.W.'s younger brother, singing in place of R.W.

5

A New Blackwood Brothers

IF YOU HAVE EVER EXPERIENCED A TRAGEDY YOU know that life is never the same afterwards. It has been said that you may get past it but you never really get over it. The tragedy of the plane crash left an indelible mark on the Blackwood family, the quartet, and gospel music as a whole.

Although I was only a year old at the time of the crash and have no conscious memory of Bill or R.W., the repercussions of that tragic day created ripples through my life, not in the sense of personal loss, but in coming to realize the effect it had on our family. R.W.'s wife, Elaine, and Bill's wife, Ruth, lost their husbands in the prime of their life. R.W.'s sons, Ron and R.W., Jr, and Bill's sons, Bill, Jr., Gary, and Curt lost their dads. Obviously, they suffered the tragedy on a level only they could fully appreciate, but the effect it had on my dad and mom was nearly as overwhelming. Daddy lost his nephew who, only two years his junior, was far more like a little brother, and also lost his best friend, Bill. He also felt the responsibility of caring for the wives and families of his fallen brothers in ministry. That he was able to regain any confidence and carry on with the group is the direct result of the prayers of many hundreds, if not thousands of people, and the sense that God was not through with the Blackwood Brothers.

I don't think my dad ever set foot in a private plane again, and they certainly were not about to resume travel in one. So, it was back to the seven-passenger limousine that was the usual mode of travel for groups at that time. The Blackwood Brothers had been the first gospel group to have their own planes, and they would also be the last.

Another immediate need for the Blackwood Brothers was finding replacements for R.W. and Bill. I can't imagine how overwhelming that task must have been. R.W. was an original member, and Bill Lyles had been with them since the mid-forties. They were an integral part of the Blackwood Brothers sound. As a musical group, your sound is what identifies you and sets you apart from everyone else. The crash took not only the lives of these two young men, but half the sound of the group as well. Already overcome with the magnitude of the loss of the two people who, other than my mom, were the closest on earth to my dad, the task of having to find someone to fill those spots must have seemed insurmountable.

R.W.'s younger brother, Cecil, seemed like a natural choice to replace R.W. Being his younger brother, fans would accept him, no questions asked. Replacing Bill would be a bit more problematic. One of the people my dad considered was a young George Younce. He also tried to find a young bass singer named Gerald Williams. Gerald had resided in Little Rock and sang with a very popular group of the day, The Melody Boys Quartet. Gerald had just left the group and, unbeknownst to my dad, moved to Iowa, feeling that was God was leading him into full-time ministry there. This was in 1954, long before the Internet and cell phones. Trying to find a number for Gerald, my dad called directory information in Little Rock. Gerald has a very smooth bass voice, much like Bill Lyles, and would have been a great fit to continue the sound the group had established. He did reach a man named Gerald Williams in Arkansas, but it was not the Gerald Williams he was seeking to find (Gerald would eventually return to Arkansas and only then learn that he had been sought out for the position of bass with the Blackwood Brothers).

Unable to connect with Gerald, my dad contacted a young bass singer who was singing with The Sunshine Boys, a popular group who, at that time, were residing in Wheeling, West Virginia. The Sunshine Boys were regulars on WWVA's program, WWVA Jamboree that ran from 1933-1997, the second longest running radio program behind the Grand Ole Opry. The Sunshine Boys were favorites on the program during the 1950s. That young bass singer's name was J.D. Sumner.

The Sunshine Boys had an interesting history as well. They began in the 1930s as a country and western band and appeared on WAGA Radio in Atlanta, Georgia. Although they had become primarily a gospel group by the time they reached WAGA, the radio station was in need of a country and western band, so the Sunshine Boys also sang as country and western artists on radio under the name of The Light Crust Dough Boys. In the mid-forties the group traveled to Hollywood and appeared as a singing group in several western films. In 1949, original members Milton 'Ace' Richman and Eddie Wallace were joined by new members Fred Daniel and J.D. Sumner and made the move to Wheeling, West Virginia. WWVA was a 50,000-watt powerhouse in the '40s, '50s and beyond, blanketing the states surrounding them and reaching even into Canada. The Sunshine Boys became regulars on WWVA's Jamboree program.

Eddie, Ace, Fred, and J.D. divided their time between Wheeling and Atlanta with occasional trips to Hollywood to pursue their movie career. In the early 1950s, the Sunshine Boys signed a major record contract with Decca Records. Their affiliation with Decca led to them to take part in one of the biggest selling recordings in gospel music history when they sang backing vocals on Red Foley's hit, "Peace in the Valley."

J.D. Sumner was enjoying a fabulous career with this group. I remember hearing the story from J.D. that he was sitting in his home in Atlanta when the news of the airplane crash came over the radio. He said he immediately had the feeling that he was going to join the Blackwood Brothers. The Blackwood Brothers and the Sunshine Boys were archrivals and there was some animosity between the groups. Within a couple of weeks my dad called him and offered him the job. He wrestled with the decision, walking the streets of Atlanta into the wee hours of the morning, unable to dismiss the offer but uncertain of leaving such a prestigious group as the Sunshine Boys. J.D. stated that when he finally talked with Ace Richman later that day, Ace told him he hated to lose him but said he'd be crazy not to go.

Thus began a new era for the Blackwood Brothers Quartet. The first concert by the new group with J.D. and Cecil was on my dad's thirty-fifth birthday, August 4th, 1954 at a Memorial Sing in Clanton, Alabama at the airfield where the crash had taken place exactly five weeks before. The charred patch in the dirt field where the plane burned was still visible. This was where the original Blackwood Brothers had nearly ended. Now it would also be the place where the new era of the group began.

J.D.'s voice was nothing like Bill Lyles. Where Bill was smooth, J.D. wasn't, but his range was very low; lower than Bill. What was unknown at the time was that J.D. would write songs; hundreds of them that would become staples in the Blackwood Brothers repertoire; songs like, "The Old Country Church," "Crossing Chilly Jordan," and "He's All That I Need" among them. J.D.'s songwriting ability was immense. When Hawaii gained statehood is 1959, my dad suggested J.D. write a Hawaiian gospel song. He didn't just write one—he wrote six! Those songs comprised half of the 1959 record called *Paradise Island*. It was a huge success and very innovative for its day. In fact, it was so successful that RCA asked the group to do a follow-up and J.D. wrote nine of the twelve songs on the 1960 release, *Beautiful Isle of Somewhere*.

His influence and creativity cannot be overstated. Traveling the highways in a seven-passenger limousine and being a full six feet, six inches tall gave him the idea of converting a bus to fit their travel needs. He presented the idea to my dad, who scoffed at it at first, but later agreed, and the tour bus was born. A replica of that first tour bus is on display at the Southern Gospel Music Hall of Fame at Dollywood Amusement Park in Pigeon Forge, Tennessee. It's not much by today's standards, but it was the first of its kind. Today, there are thousands of tour busses in use by musicians in every genre of music, a testimony to the vision and foresight of J.D. Sumner.

J.D.'s songs and his on-stage antics became a highlight of the reformed Blackwood Brothers Quartet. He was larger than life. His incredible ability to sing low combined with his huge persona made him a crowd favorite. The Blackwood Brothers Quartet entered a new era with the addition of J.D. to the group. They would never be the same after the crash but what they became was no less spectacular. From the mid-fifties to the mid-sixties they would fill concert halls across the United States and Canada with their lively brand of gospel quartet music.

Within two years of J.D. and Cecil joining the Blackwood Brothers, they were invited back to appear on *Arthur Godfrey's Talent Scouts* program and they won again singing a song called "The Good Book." Like a phoenix rising from the ashes, the Blackwood Brothers would soar to even greater heights!

Eddie Wallace, JD Sumner,
Ace Richman, Fred Daniel - circa 1950

The Sunshine Boys, 1950

Ed Wallace, Fred Daniel,
Ace Richman, JD Sumner
on the set of Prairie Roundup, circa 1953

The Sunshine Boys on a western movie set, 1953

The newly reformed BBQ, l-r Bill Shaw, James, Cecil, and J.D. Sumner singing bass.

A group picture before acquiring matching suits, top row Bill Shaw, Jackie Marshall, James, bottom row, Cecil, J.D. Sumner, late 1954

The 'New' BBQ in concert, 1955

A new promo picture, 1956

The first ever tour bus!

Recliners in a bus; what a concept!

6

The Statesmen Quartet

It is impossible to tell the story of the Blackwood Brothers history without mentioning their partnership with the Statesmen Quartet of Atlanta, Georgia. Any true fan of gospel quartet music history would most likely be aware of the team of the Blackwood Brothers and The Statesmen. As a performing team, these two groups established gospel quartet music as a powerful entertaining force. They filled auditoriums across the South and eventually pioneered most of the continental United States and Canada with their lively stage presentation and concert showmanship.

My dad had the idea of forming a team with another quartet; one that was different in style and presentation than were the Blackwood Brothers. His vision was to have both groups appear in concert, and to foster the idea that there was competition between them. He somehow realized the appeal of such an arrangement. His first choice for a partner was not the Statesmen! His first choice was his friend, Smilin' Joe Roper and the Melody Boys from Little Rock, Arkansas. He presented the idea to Joe, who apparently failed to see the potential of the idea. Undeterred by Joe's rejection, he then approached Hovie Lister, the manager of the Statesmen Quartet, and the rest, as they say, is history.

In addition to their professional partnership, lifelong friendships were born out of this alliance, particularly with my dad, J.D. Sumner, Jake Hess and Hovie Lister. Some of my earliest memories are our family's annual summer vacations at the beach on Jekyll Island, Georgia. My dad and mom, J.D. and Mary, Jake and Joyce, and Hovie and Ethel with kids in tow, frolicked along the shores of the Atlantic Ocean one week every August in this picturesque locale.

J.D. and Mary's daughters, Frances and Shirley, were my brother Jimmy's age, but Jake and Joyce's children, Becky and Chris, and Hovie and Ethel's kids, Lisa and Chip, were more my age and we made some great memories playing at the beach during those years. Jake and Joyce's youngest, Jake, Jr., was just a baby at the time, and we didn't really become friends until much later. "Little Jake," as he was called, is the husband of Judy Martin of the Martins.

Remember, it was the Statesmen who were sharing the concert with the Blackwood Brothers at the Chilton County Peach Festival in Clanton, Alabama on June 30, 1954, the day of the plane crash. They stood and saw the plane fall to the ground, instantly killing R.W. and Bill. It was Jake Hess who took off running after my dad, bear hugging him from behind, preventing him from running into the flaming wreckage and possibly saving his life in the process. It was the Statesmen who drove my dad and the other members of the group back to Memphis that evening. They attended the funeral of their fallen friends. When they began resuming concert appearances, their bass singer, Jim "Big Chief" Wetherington, filled in with the Blackwood Brothers. These guys and their families were very close friends. So, spending summer vacations together was a natural outgrowth of their friendships.

These two groups set the standard for gospel quartet concerts. After the Blackwood Brothers won *Arthur Godfrey's Talent Scouts*, the Statesmen made an appearance on the program and won singing Stuart Hamblen's song "This Ol' House." Both groups had benefitted tremendously from this national television exposure in a time when there were only three TV channels and *Talent Scouts* was the most popular program in America.

Concert halls were sold out across the South and eventually into Southern California and up the West Coast. In the 1950s, many church folks didn't approve of most secular entertainment, many didn't go to movie theaters, and their social calendars were pretty bare. Gospel quartet music, although shunned by some very conservative Christians as too worldly, nonetheless won the hearts of much of the churched world. *Talent Scouts* had made these guys stars, but stars with a wholesome gospel message that was congruent with the beliefs of most Christians.

For reasons unknown to me, I have always been called by nicknames by those closest to me. I don't know if these friends of my dad, having known me practically from birth, heard me say something or where the phrase originated, but my nickname among these guys was Be-bump. Jake, Joyce, J.D. and Mary all called me Be-bump literally till the day they died.

My point in sharing this little tidbit is definitely not to resurrect the usage of this nickname, but to make the point that we only call someone a nickname when we are in very close relationship. The fact that these friends and partners of my dad were on such close terms that calling one of their kids by a nickname known to all of them simply points to the closeness they and their families enjoyed.

One of my earliest memories was attending the funeral of Denver Crumpler, the tenor singer for the Statesmen Quartet before Rosie Rozell joined the group. The year was 1957. I was four years old. The funeral was in Atlanta, and I recall us driving through the cemetery. As I remember, it was in a beautiful hilly setting.

The Blackwood Brothers and Statesmen did hundreds, if not thousands, of concerts together. They recorded Christmas records together. They produced an early TV program called *Singing Time In Dixie* together, and formed a record company together. They even bought matching busses and had them painted identically. The only difference was the names on the scroll on the side of the busses. Their partnership was unparalleled and enjoyed great success. There have been and continue to be group partnerships in gospel music and, for the most part, these partnerships are great for our industry and for the groups involved. But they all go back to the Blackwood Brothers and the Statesmen. They were the first to present it on anything near the scale they achieved.

This was the era in which I grew up. As I think back to my childhood, there are many memories of concert halls such as Ellis Auditorium in Memphis, Boutwell Auditorium in Birmingham, Municipal Auditorium in Atlanta, Will Rogers Auditorium in Ft. Worth, and many others. When I went with my dad to his work, these are the places I visited along with countless school auditoriums and churches across the country. The education I received by traveling to these cities provided me an invaluable look into the life and culture of our nation through a very unique lens.

I met hundreds of people who were of my dad's generation, who watched me grow up from a kid to a teenager to an adult and who welcomed me into their lives, and it has been one of the most satisfying aspects of my life to count as friends people who are older than I am, whose names I would never know and with whom I would have no relationship if it were not for my dad and their friendships.

The Statesmen were just one set of friends in this category. As a gospel music brat, if you will, I grew to have wonderful relationships with the Speer Family, the Oak Ridge Boys, the Rambos, the Hemphills, the Florida Boys, the Dixie Echoes, and the list goes on and on. Add to those the fans and friends who welcomed me into their lives and I can't help but think how blessed I am to have known so many wonderful people in my life.

One of those was a man so special to me I have to give him his own chapter. But first...

The Statesmen Quartet of my childhood (late 50s – early 60s)

The Team of the Blackwood Brothers & The Statesmen Quartet

7

THE BLACKWOOD 'LITTLE' BROTHERS

THERE WAS A VERY MUSICAL FAMILY IN MEMPHIS named The Pilants. Verle and Marge had three sons, Gary, Doug, and Greg, and they sang around Memphis. I'm not sure how our families met, but we discovered that Verle taught voice and Marge taught piano. My dad and Cecil arranged for Mark, Cecil's son, and me to take voice lessons from Verle and piano lessons from Marge.

The Pilant brothers were close in age to Mark and me and we soon developed a good friendship with them. It wasn't long before we were singing with the Pilant Brothers, and it seemed to make sense to our dads to form a quartet. How we did that with five of us I don't quite remember (I think Gary played piano some of the time, although his mom played for us as well). Anyway, form a quartet we did. And, though there were three Pilants and two Blackwoods, the decision was made to call us the Blackwood 'Little' Brothers!

My brother, Jimmy, by that time, was singing with R.W. Blackwood, Jr., and Bill Lyles, Jr., in a group called, The Junior Blackwood Brothers. Jim Brown sang tenor, and Everett Reece played piano. They had released an album on Skylite appropriately called *Songs Our Fathers Sang*. Bill Lyles, Jr. was later replaced by Phil Enloe, whose brother, Neil, was with the Couriers.

In 1964, the Blackwood Brothers recorded an album called *The Blackwood Family Album* on which both the Junior Blackwoods and the Blackwood Little Brothers performed some of the songs. The Blackwood Little Brothers were featured on "This Little Light Of Mine" and "The Devil's Gonna Get You If You Don't Watch Out."

Verle and Marge would drive their boys, and my mom and Cecil's wife, Doris, would drive Mark and me to our concerts. I was the emcee for the group, mimicking what I had seen my dad do countless times. Gary, the oldest of us, was only twelve or thirteen, and Greg, the youngest, was six or seven. We dressed in matching suits and sang in some major concerts in the early sixties. Audiences ate it up! I remember one Christmas we were filming a television program at WHBQ in Memphis. I was introducing the next song we were singing and couldn't recall the title! Verle Pilant, our vocal coach, was kneeling by the cameras in front of us to remind us to smile, etc. He quickly realized I was blank on the title and mouthed it to me. It was "Go Tell It on The Mountain." That footage would be priceless but is, fortunately or unfortunately, long gone!

One of the highlights of our young career was recording in Sun Studios in Memphis, where Elvis and Johnny Cash and Jerry Lee Lewis and Carl Perkins had recorded their early records. We eventually called it quits, but not before we took these pictures.

The Blackwood Little Brothers, top row, l-r, Doug Pilant, Gary Pilant, Greg Pilant, Bottom row, l-r, Billy Blackwood, Mark Blackwood

Our primitive mode of transportation

Recording in Sam Phillips Studio in Memphis, circa 1963

8

J. D. Sumner

J.D. Sumner was born in Lakeland, Florida on November 19, 1924. He would grow to be six feet, six inches tall, and cast an immeasurably large shadow over the gospel music world. In addition to being a phenomenal gospel singer, J.D. was a prolific songwriter, and a pioneer in the Gospel music field. He sang in five quartets and was a member of the Blackwood Brothers Quartet during their 1950s and 1960s heyday. Aside from his incredibly low bass voice, his business acumen helped promote Southern Gospel Quartet music and move it into the mainstream of American culture and music during the '50s and '60s.

J.D. joined the Blackwood Brothers in the summer of 1954 shortly after the plane crash that claimed the lives of R.W. Blackwood and Bill Lyles. As I wrote in Chapter Four, he joined the group at a time when the fresh memory of that horrific day cast a pall over the Blackwood family, friends and fans. In hindsight it is probably a good thing that J.D. sounded nothing like Bill Lyles. They were both tall, both funny, and both charismatic, but their voices were nothing alike. Where Bill was smooth as silk, J.D. wasn't, but he could sing lower than most any human on the planet.

I was eighteen months old when J.D. joined the Blackwood Brothers, so I never knew anything but J.D. He and my dad became the closest of friends as well as business partners. As already stated, what was unknown at the time he joined the group was the wealth of songs and genius ideas that came along with his incredible voice. It was his idea to customize a bus for travel, his idea to formalize the idea of a convention for quartets, and his idea, along with my dad, to establish an organization for the promotion of gospel music, known as the Gospel Music Association.

Over the years he became like my second dad. As a kid traveling on the bus, J.D. was someone I looked up to—way up to! My dad was five feet, five inches while J.D. was six feet, six inches; taller than anyone else in my world. And he treated me as if he really was my second dad. In fact, I have a large glossy of J.D. he autographed to me that says, "There's only one thing I don't like about you; you're not my son (but in my heart you are)."

In 1964 my dad, his nephew, Cecil, and J.D. bought the Stamps Quartet Music Company from Frank Stamps, inheriting the name "Stamps Quartet" along with it. They formed a new Stamps Quartet comprised of "Big" John Hall, Roger McDuff, Terry Blackwood, Jerry Redd, and "Smiling" Joe Roper on piano. My understanding is that they bought the company for the publishing rights to the vast Stamps catalog, and that the quartet was kind of an add-on.

In the next three years Jerry Redd would be replaced by Jim Hill, Terry Blackwood would be replaced by Mylon LeFevre, who would soon be replaced by my brother, Jimmy Blackwood, and Chuck Ramsey would replace Joe Roper. J.D.'s nephew, Donnie, would soon take over piano for Chuck, but shortly thereafter move to lead singer to replace Roger McDuff. Their 1964 LP releases *What A Day That Will Be*, written by member Jim Hill, and *Without Him*, written by Mylon LeFevre, became timeless classics that can now be found in most modern hymnbooks.

In 1965 my dad and J.D. came to the realization they couldn't successfully manage the Stamps from afar, and the decision was made for J.D. to move to the Stamps and bring "Big" John Hall to the Blackwood Brothers. This would prove to be a huge move for both groups. Shortly thereafter, my brother Jimmy joined the Stamps on baritone, Donnie Sumner moved from piano to lead, Jim Hill continued as tenor, and J.D. hired a kid from North Carolina named Tony Brown to play piano, and a young guitarist named Jimmy "Duke" Dumas to play lead guitar. After a brief stint with his family, Mylon LeFevre returned to play bass guitar.

That was the Stamps Quartet of 1967, the first year I traveled with them playing drums. Actually, I was just playing drum— a snare drum. Just a snare drum. In retrospect it seems silly, but in 1967 a live drummer in a gospel quartet was a relatively new idea. The Imperials had just started using a drummer, Larry Benson, but they were on the cutting edge of contemporary gospel music. Also, for a brief time, Greg Gordon, son of Chuck Wagon Gang's Anna Gordon, played drums with the Oak Ridge Boys.

J.D. got away with having a drummer because, number one, he was J.D. and he could get away with things others couldn't, and because I was fourteen years old and only playing a snare drum. It was a novelty; what can I say? It was what it was. That was the summer between my eighth and ninth grade years of high school. Going back to school at the end of that summer was torture. I had been bitten by the traveling musician bug and knew where I was headed.

After much pleading and begging during the following school year, my dad relented to let me join the Stamps and finish my high schooling by correspondence. So, in the summer of 1968 I joined J.D. and the Stamps playing drums, or, well, drum. It wasn't long before my snare drum was joined by a full trap set and I was off and running.

So, now my dad's best friend and business partner was my boss. My year-and-a-half in the Stamps was quite an experience, and more fun than a human being should be allowed to have. In the acquisition of the Stamps Music Company my dad, Cecil, and J.D. also inherited the Stamps School of Music, a three-week music school held every June in Dallas to promote gospel music and initiate young people wanting to get into the industry in the fundamentals of singing, playing, reading music and harmonizing. For a fourteen-year-old kid the music school was like summer camp on steroids. Because of my position with the Stamps, and the fact that James Blackwood was my dad, I had instant celebrity status, which would turn out to not be a good thing, but for the moment it was very exciting.

The prologue to this book tells a story in which we pushed the Stamps' bus over what seemed like much of downtown Ft. Worth, Texas one night. I realize that may not seem like fun, but when you're fifteen and you're elbow-to-elbow with guys older than you are, and you're all up to your eyeballs in grease, pushing a fifteen-ton bus, there's a sense of belonging that accompanies those kinds of events.

At the 1968 Stamps School, which had moved to Waxahachie, Texas, there was a young musician from Michigan named Tim Baty. Tim and I instantly hit it off and played countless games of ping-pong in the Student Union Building that school term. Tim was a budding bass guitarist and landed a job playing with the Stamps. Mylon had left to pursue a solo career in Christian rock and had left an opening that Tim walked into and made his own. Tim was not only a good bass player, but also a good singer and would eventually be a third of the group, Voice, with Donnie Sumner and Sherrill Nielsen. More on that later...

J.D. had a bus full of young guys, some of whom had no business being away from home, but there we were in all our glory, traveling 250 days a year all over the U.S. and Canada, having the time of our lives.

J. D. Sumner, circa 1960

The BBQ in the mid-to-late 50s, l-r Jack Marshall, James, Bill Shaw, Cecil, J. D. Sumner in one of the many appearances in support of Youth for Christ

BBQ promo picture, circa 1960, clockwise from lower left, Wally Varner, pianist, Cecil, Bill Shaw, James, and J. D. Sumner

The Stamps Quartet on stage at NQC, Memphis, 1967 (me on drums)

The Stamps Quartet promo picture, 1969, standing, l-r, Roy McNeil, J. D. Sumner, Donnie Sumner, Jimmy Blackwood, sitting, l-r, Tim Baty, me, Tony Brown, Duke Dumas

The Stamps Band, clockwise from left, me, Tim Baty, Duke Dumas, Tony Brown

Me with my snare drum, circa, 1967

J. D.'s autographed picture to me

9

Gospel Drums

As a kid, I had the privilege of traveling with my dad on many occasions. I believe I was about five or six years old when all the families boarded the Blackwood Brothers bus and headed to California for a three-week tour. One of the highlights of that trip was a visit with Roy Rogers and Dale Evans at their ranch near Apple Valley, California. Practically my only memory of that entire trip was the few moments I got to sit atop Roy's famous horse, Trigger. My childhood was punctuated with trips to various locales around the country and great memories with my dad.

By far, the most adventurous trip ever with my parents was in June of 1968. The Blackwood Brothers were taking a group of fans and friends on an eighteen-day trip to the Holy Land and the capitals of Europe. The itinerary included London, Paris, Rome, Athens, Berlin, Stockholm, Edinburgh, The Hague, Amsterdam and Rotterdam, and seven days in Israel. I was fifteen and it was a life-changing experience for me; one I'll never forget. Among the most memorable sites were the Berlin Wall, being escorted through Checkpoint Charlie, seeing the Tower of London, the Eiffel Tower, a castle in Edinburgh, the Colosseum in Rome, and the Parthenon in Athens. But the most moving experiences were in Israel—the Via Dolorosa, Golgotha and the Garden Tomb. I have never had the privilege of returning to Israel or most of those capitals but the memories will always be with me.

Upon arriving back home, I was off to the Stamps School of Music in Waxahachie, Texas, and the beginning of my full-time touring gig with the Stamps. Being with the Stamps was, as earlier stated, more fun than a human should be allowed to have. I've already shared how much I looked up to J.D., and my big brother, Jimmy, was also a hero of mine. To be on the bus with them and Donnie Sumner, Jim Hill, Tony Brown, Mylon LeFevre, and Duke Dumas was an unbelievable experience. I was living the dream, at fifteen! The Stamps were a very popular group, traveling the major concert circuit and playing to great audiences across the US and Canada.

My first real performance on drums was for a solo record daddy did on RCA Victor records. It was about 1967 and I had no business being on the session. RCA was a major company and this was a major record. Bill Walker, the designated session leader and arranger was playing piano, Harold Bradley was playing acoustic rhythm guitar, Wayne Moss was playing electric guitar and Roy Huskey, Jr., was playing upright bass. These guys were among the top players in Nashville, and the only reason I was even in the room was because it was my dad's record. We were recording in Nashville at RCA, Studio A. I was petrified but lived through it somehow. Meeting those guys and playing on a session with them was amazing! I later developed a dear friendship with Wayne Moss and we laughed about the day we first met there at RCA Studio A.

In the summer of '69 my dad began to have some health issues. He was still leading the Blackwood Brothers and maintaining a rigorous touring schedule at age fifty. Although fifty is not very old, when you've spent thirty-five of those years on the road, your body begins to complain. While a tour bus is a convenient and relatively comfortable means of transportation, there is truly no place like home and your own bed. Anyone who has traveled for a living will tell you that travel is physically taxing. Add to it the work of hauling in and setting up equipment, performing the concert, tearing the equipment back down and loading it, and you have a pretty full day of work.

As my dad's health began to be a challenge, he thought bringing Jimmy into the Blackwood Brothers would allow him to take a back seat and get some needed rest. That was a rational and wise decision, but it had the unintended consequence of meaning I, too, would leave the Stamps and join the Blackwood Brothers to play drums. It didn't seem right to my dad to leave me in the Stamps at sixteen years old without my big brother there to watch over me. While that decision made perfect sense, I wasn't thrilled with leaving the Stamps. The Blackwood Brothers were much more traditional in their song selection and performance style and I was a teenager with anything but "traditional" on my mind. But, I really had no choice in the matter and on December 11, 1969 I played my first concert with the Blackwood Brothers in Pryor, Oklahoma. The reason I remember it so vividly is that I stepped off the bus in my suit preparing to enter the auditorium for our concert when I heard the group singing the first song. I had somehow misunderstood the time for the concert and I was late for my very first concert as a member of the Blackwood Brothers! I'll never forget the look on my dad's face as I snuck in behind the drum set and began playing. It was not a pleasant way to start my new job!

While I tried to adjust to playing drums with the Blackwood Brothers, there was other music playing in my head. I had been swept up in the popular music of the day, namely, the Beatles and others who had caught my musical ear with the records they were making. In fact, although I had taken piano lessons for a number of years, the Beatles had inspired me to take up guitar and drums and were directly responsible for the career I had chosen of being a professional drummer. By the time I made the transition to the Blackwood Brothers at the end of 1969, I was, unbeknownst to my dad, listening to a lot of secular music on my headphones in my bunk on the bus as we were riding down the roads of America. Every night in concert I'd play drums to "The Old Country Church" and "Camping in Canaan's Land," then get on the bus and listen to everything coming out on the pop charts. They two styles could not have been much more divergent and I could not have been much more frustrated.

 I don't want to paint a negative picture of my time as a drummer with the Blackwood Brothers. There were a lot of great things that happened during those years. One of them was when we were invited to appear on a Johnny Cash TV special featuring Billy Graham. It was 1971 and Johnny was pursuing a closer relationship with the Lord and wanted to produce a very God-honoring TV special. In addition to Dr. Graham and the Blackwood Brothers, the Staple Singers, a black gospel family group, were on the program as well. One of my biggest disappointments happened during the filming. We stopped to take a picture on the set with Johnny. Our bass player, Larry Davis, was nowhere to be found. I took off to find him and that's when they took the picture! You'll see the photo at the end of this chapter and if you look really hard you'll see where I would have been standing right by my dad and Johnny Cash!

 We won two of our seven Grammy Awards in those years, for *L-O-V-E* in 1972 and *Release Me* (From My Sin) in 1973. Being a member of the group and the drummer on those records I got to take a Grammy Award home each of those years.

One event etched in my memory happened in New York City. We were in concert in the area and had a day off. It was in late November or early December as best as I recall. Radio City Music Hall was staging their annual Christmas program and daddy asked if I'd like to go. The Christmas program began there in 1933 and has run every holiday season since then. The famous Rockettes and the great Wurlitzer organ are year-round features of the great performance hall, but in November and December the Christmas spectacular becomes the focal point. I was actually unaware of this fact when my dad and I went there that day. We sat through the first half performance of the Rockettes dancing and the orchestra playing through a fabulous presentation of traditional Christmas carols, but the real showstopper was after intermission.

The lights dimmed and the curtain rose to reveal a manger scene complete with live animals. The story of Jesus' birth and life was acted out on the stage before us in a breathtaking performance and ended with the poem "One Solitary Life," scrolling from bottom to top on a scrim as the characters and animals remained in view upstage. If you aren't familiar with the poem, I have included it below. My dad and I sat there in tears at the beauty and majesty of this celebration of the life of our Lord Jesus. My understanding is that, although some of the components of the show have changed over the years, the second half production of the life of Jesus, complete with animals and the "One Solitary Life" poem remains.

"One Solitary Life"
James Allan Francis (1864–1928)

He was born in an obscure village
The son of a peasant woman
He grew up in another obscure village
Where He worked with His father in a carpenter shop
until He was thirty
Then for three years He was an itinerant preacher
He never wrote a book
He never held an office
He never went to college
He never visited a big city
He never travelled more than two hundred miles
from the place where He was born
He did none of the things
usually associated with greatness
He had no credentials but Himself
He was only thirty-three
when the tide of public opinion turned against Him
His friends ran away
One of them denied Him
He was turned over to His enemies
And went through the mockery of a trial
He was nailed to a cross between two thieves
While dying, his executioners gambled for His clothing,
the only property He had on earth
When He was dead
He was laid in a borrowed grave
through the pity of a friend
Twenty centuries have come and gone
And yet today He is the central figure of the human race

And the leader of mankind's progress
All the armies that have ever marched
All the navies that have ever sailed
All the parliaments that have ever sat
All the kings that ever reigned put together
Have not affected the life of mankind on earth
As much as that one solitary life

 As anyone with artistic creativity will tell you, the desire to create is a powerful force, particularly when coupled with youthful zeal. I was scratching the itch to travel and play music on one level, but the music was not engaging or challenging to me to say the least. So, I sought to find a way to work within the confines of the Blackwood Brothers while simultaneously pursuing my musical tastes. My first attempt was a 45rpm single. On one side was an instrumental "song" I composed called "Gospel Drums." Side B was a song I had heard Mylon LeFevre sing called "You Were on His Mind," in which I sang and played acoustic guitar. Both were, in hindsight, relatively poor attempts to scratch my musical itch, but at the time I was desperate for a creative outlet that sounded like the music in my head.

 I think some explanation is necessary at this point to help anyone not alive in the sixties understand the cultural upheaval that took place in our country. Every generation seeks its own answers and the 1960s experienced a cultural upheaval of epic proportions. I was right on the cusp of that revolution and found myself trying to keep one foot in the past and one foot in the future, which proved to be impossible. Musically speaking, the British Invasion of music into American culture had a profound effect on young people, myself included. The fifties was the decade of Elvis and Pat Boone,

Fabian, and Annette Funicello, but in the sixties the Beatles and other British groups impacted the youth culture like a tidal wave.

At the same time, there was a heightened interest in spiritual things and some of the music reflected that dynamic. Songs like "Let It Be," "Bridge Over Troubled Water," "Get Together," "Turn, Turn, Turn," and others seemed to search for an answer to age-old questions in a new way. And those songs felt more authentic to me than many of the songs I had heard growing up in church. Please understand I am not defending as much as I am explaining. Anyone who was at least ten years old in the sixties can attest to the musical apple cart turnover that was taking place on American radio.

Lest I lose you at this point, let me state I am now a true champion of old songs and hymns. In the current Blackwood Brothers Quartet, of which I am the leader and the musical director, one of our latest CDs includes ten classic gospel songs such as "He Touched Me," and "What A Day That Will Be." Our latest CD is an a cappella hymn project. I have come full circle with respect to the validity of great old songs, but to be honest there were some songs I sang while growing up that were antiquated well before I was born and frankly were not very good songs to begin with.

After my initial single record of "Gospel Drums," I released an LP (that stands for Long Playing for you who don't remember vinyl) with cover versions of the four songs I mentioned above, "Let It Be," "Bridge Over Troubled Water," "Get Together," and "Turn, Turn, Turn," as well as two Ray Stevens songs, "Everything Is Beautiful," and "A Brighter Day." I then recorded another single with a song I wrote called, "Reflections," and a 'B' side of "Come Back Home." They were the first two songs from another LP called *One Way*. Many of my gospel music friends came to Memphis to help me on this second record, including Reba Rambo, Tony Brown, Marc and Suzan Speer, Curt Lyles, John Rich, and Steve Sanders. Neither of those records was worth the vinyl they were pressed on. They were terrible recordings and nothing more than self-indulgent attempts at musical authenticity by a young searching soul.

It was not long after this record that I began to dabble in drugs. Many of my friends were already experimenting with marijuana and, although I had declared I would not follow suit, I soon became a part of the drug culture. This alienated me from my dad and mom, who were watching with fear and frustration as I began to drift away from them. I would often have pot with me on the road and snuck around to hide my growing addiction to smoking it. Unable to reconcile my musical and personal disconnect, I made the decision to leave the Blackwood Brothers. My final concert was to be in Nashville at 1973 National Quartet Convention. My dad was heartbroken at my decision and was concerned about the direction my life was taking. And who could blame him!

The BBQ & Band, circa, 1970, clockwise from lower left, Peter Kaups, pianist, me, Bill Shaw, Cecil, Jimmy, London Parris, Larry Davis, bass guitarist, Dwayne Friend, guitarist, and James (seated)

The BBQ with Roy Rogers & Dale Evans, circa 1972

The BBQ, circa, 1973, top row, l-r, me, Tommy Fairchild, pianist, Ken Turner, Jimmy, Larry Davis, bass guitarist, seated, l-r, James, Bill Shaw, Cecil

The BBQ on the Johnny Cash Special, November 1971, l-r, Peter Kaups, James, Bill Shaw, Johnny Cash, Jimmy, Cecil, London Parris

James with Billy Graham & Johnny Cash, November 1971

The BBQ appearing at the Billy Graham Crusade in Memphis, 1977, l-r, James, Jimmy, Pat Hoffmaster, Billy Graham, Ken Turner, Cecil

The BBQ receiving a Grammy award, 1972, l-r, James, Cecil, Bill Shaw, me, Larry Davis, Peter Kaups

Me at the drums on stage, circa, 1971

Me at the drums, unknown location, circa, 1973

Recording my second solo record at a studio in J. D. Sumner's home in Memphis, circa, 1972, back row, l-r, Art Beard, Marc Speer, Suzan Speer, Judy Breland, Steve Sanders, Peter Kaups, Curt Lyles, Mark Goodman, middle row, l-r, me, unknown girl, bottom row, l-r, Tony Brown, Reba Rambo

10

Elvis and the Blackwood Brothers

There are probably very few human beings over forty who don't know who Elvis Presley is. Maybe in Mongolia or somewhere in Africa, but it is a fact that no entertainer of any genre has impacted music and culture on a global scale more than Elvis Presley. What most of his fans probably don't know is that the Blackwood Brothers were one of his earliest and biggest influences.

As I mentioned in chapter three, the Presleys lived in a housing complex in downtown Memphis called Lauderdale Courts. This was just a few blocks from the Ellis Auditorium, the largest concert venue in Memphis and the location of monthly gospel concerts hosted by the Blackwood Brothers beginning shortly after their move there in 1950. It is an acknowledged fact that Elvis came to as many of those concerts as his truck-driving salary would allow.

It is also a fact that the Presleys attended First Assembly of God Church on McLemore Avenue, which was also the home church of the Blackwoods. The quartet would sing at church on occasion when their travel schedule allowed them the opportunity to be home on a Sunday. So, Elvis and his mom and dad were very much aware of the quartet and Elvis became a fan at a young age.

At the Ellis Auditorium he would have been exposed to a number of gospel groups of the day, most notably the Statesmen, who were arguably his favorite group. The Speer Family, The Oak Ridge Quartet (The Oak Ridge Boys in their pre-country days), the Prophets and many others graced the stage of the Ellis during that era. Elvis's musical style was greatly influenced by the gospel music he heard both at the Ellis and at First Assembly. In fact, when he began recording he enlisted the services of the Jordanaires, a gospel quartet in Nashville who had established a career as backup singers on Nashville recording sessions.

Elvis also recorded entire gospel records early in his career, with *His Hand in Mine* and *How Great Thou Art* being the first two of those records. I find it extremely interesting that of all the million selling singles and records of his career, Elvis won only three Grammy awards, and those were not for "Blue Suede Shoes," "Heartbreak Hotel," "Suspicious Minds" or any of his secular songs or records. All three were awarded him for his gospel recordings—the first in 1967 for his second gospel record, *How Great Thou Art*, then in 1972 for his third gospel record *He Touched Me*, and again in 1974 for a live recording of *How Great Thou Art*.

As a kid I remember Elvis coming to the concerts in Memphis after he had achieved stardom. He never lost his love for gospel music and would often attend the concerts at the Ellis. At this point in his life and career he would be ushered in secretly and sit back stage, watching and listening from the wings to the music he so dearly loved. At other times he would call my dad and ask if "the guys" were in town and, if so, could they come out to Graceland and sing. On several occasions I recall my dad leaving to go out to spend the evening and usually into the wee hours of the morning sitting around the piano at Graceland, Elvis playing and singing songs as they harmonized.

On one occasion I remember my dad getting a call and, upon hanging up the phone, told me Elvis had called and invited him out to Graceland to see his baby girl, Lisa Marie. Elvis had great respect for my dad and always called him Mr. Blackwood, and apparently wanted to share the joy of his firstborn with my dad. My dad asked if I wanted to go and I said, "Sure, I'd love to!" So, we hopped in the car and drove to Graceland, about a twenty-minute drive to the south side of Memphis. When we arrived, someone met us at the door and ushered us into the foyer where we waited. In just a few minutes Elvis came down the steps from the second floor holding Lisa Marie in his arms. She was still a tiny baby at the time. I don't recall if my dad held her but I remember thinking how cool it was to be witnessing the relationship Elvis had with him. Elvis held him in high regard and he was proud to be showing off his baby girl to one of his earliest musical heroes. I had no idea at the time, but in just a few years I would be spending quite a bit of time around Elvis, traveling with the Elvis Presley Show and opening for the king himself!

The relationship between Elvis and the Blackwood Brothers is well documented. The Blackwood Brothers were Gladys Presley's favorite gospel artist. When she passed away, Elvis and Vernon chartered a plane to retrieve the guys from their tour in North Carolina to come to Memphis to sing at her funeral.

This is from www.Graceland.com:

> "August 8, 1958: Gladys Presley becomes ill and returns to Memphis via train to be hospitalized with acute hepatitis. Elvis is granted emergency leave and arrives in Memphis on the afternoon of August 12. He visits her that night, and the next day and night. A few hours after Elvis goes home to Graceland to rest, she dies in the early hours of August 14 at age 46. Her body lies in state at Graceland that afternoon. Services are at the Memphis Funeral Home on the 15, with

the Blackwood Brothers singing 'Precious Memories' and 'Rock of Ages,' two of Gladys Presley's favorite hymns. She is laid to rest at Forest Hill Cemetery, close to Graceland. Elvis is devastated."

Elvis's love for gospel music is also well documented. And he especially loved gospel quartet music! When, in 1969, he went to Las Vegas for a series of shows at the Hilton International he asked the Imperials to be part of his stage show. The Imperials, formed originally by gospel music legend Jake Hess, had established themselves as one of the premier groups in our industry. When they landed the gig with Elvis, the group included Armond Morales, Jim Murray, my cousin Terry Blackwood, Joe Moscheo on piano, and four guys singing baritone during those years: Dave Will, Greg Gordon, Roger Wiles and Sherman Andrus.

One night in Elvis's suite after a performance, Elvis asked the Imperials to sing a song for him and they began singing an a cappella version of Doris Akers's great song, "Sweet, Sweet Spirit." After that night he wanted it sung every night in concert. When the Imperials left the show and the Stamps took their place, the Stamps learned the same arrangement and sang it in nearly every show as well. I had heard that his favorite song of all time was "How Great Thou Art." That song was also in every show, and he was obviously giving an opportunity for God to be glorified at that point in the concert. Without fail, "How Great Thou Art" was one of the highlights of the program.

Someone once yelled out during a show, "Elvis, you're the king!" to which he replied, "I am not the king. Jesus Christ is the King. I'm just an entertainer." That pretty much sums up Elvis to me. He recognized he had been given a gift and, although one might disagree with how he used that gift, it was obvious to anyone who knew him that he believed in God and gave Him glory for the talent he had been given.

Elvis backstage at the Ellis Auditorium in Memphis, circa, 1955, l-r, Jack Marshall, Doyle Blackwood, Elvis Presley, James, Bill Shaw, Cecil, J. D. Sumner

Elvis with his heroes, circa 1970, l-r, James Blackwood, Hovie Lister, Elvis Presley, J. D. Sumner

"Over The Next Hill We'll Be Home" sheet music, composed by Johnny Cash

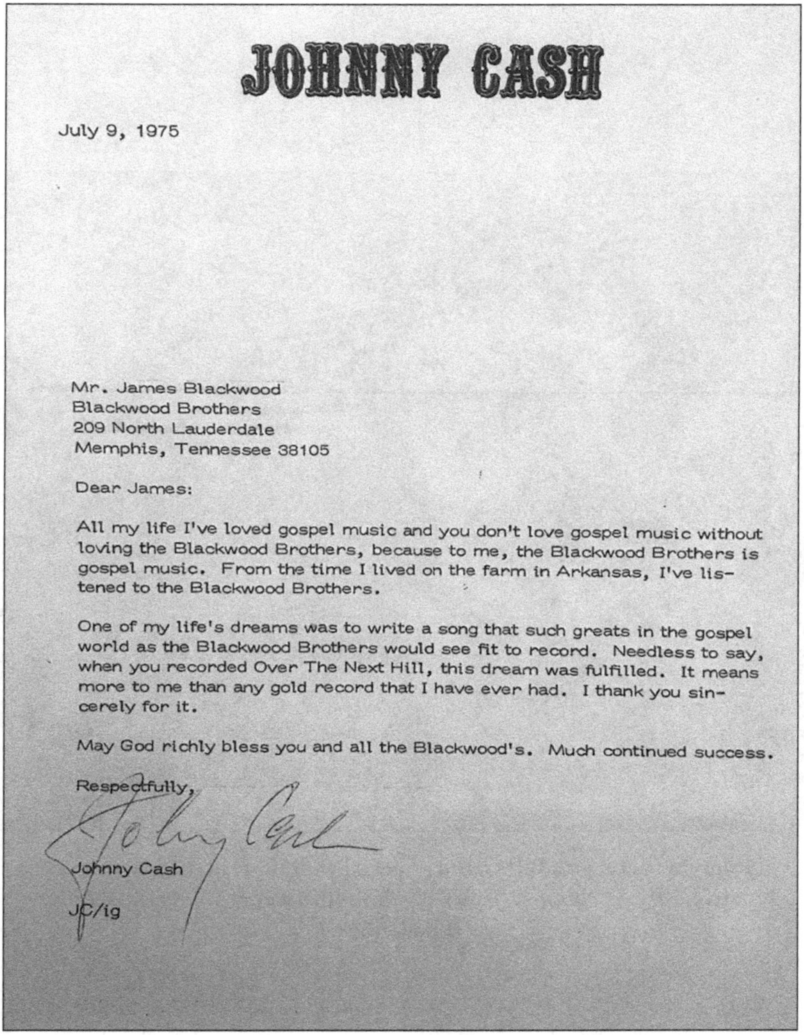

JOHNNY CASH

July 9, 1975

Mr. James Blackwood
Blackwood Brothers
209 North Lauderdale
Memphis, Tennessee 38105

Dear James:

All my life I've loved gospel music and you don't love gospel music without loving the Blackwood Brothers, because to me, the Blackwood Brothers is gospel music. From the time I lived on the farm in Arkansas, I've listened to the Blackwood Brothers.

One of my life's dreams was to write a song that such greats in the gospel world as the Blackwood Brothers would see fit to record. Needless to say, when you recorded Over The Next Hill, this dream was fulfilled. It means more to me than any gold record that I have ever had. I thank you sincerely for it.

May God richly bless you and all the Blackwood's. Much continued success.

Respectfully,

Johnny Cash

Johnny Cash

JC/ig

Johnny Cash letter to James Blackwood upon his learning that the BBQ had recorded his song, July 1975

Tammy Wynette on a Bill Gaither Special with three of the Masters Five Quartet, l-r, J. D. Sumner, James Blackwood, Tammy Wynette, Jake Hess, Bill Gaither

July 14, 1994

James Blackwood
4411 Sequoia Road
Memphis, TN 38117

Dear James:

We finally received 8X10's from the taping and I hope you will enjoy these two pictures.

James, I am so grateful for your friendship through the years. It brings me such joy to call on all my memories of you and the Blackwood Brothers. Your music was such a force in my young years and to this day I rejoice when I hear you sing. You helped make that night at TNN Studios another great and wonderful memory.

All my love to you and Miriam.

Tammy

TW/mg

Tammy Wynette letter to my dad after this TV special

The Statler Brothers record album, Thank You, World, 1974

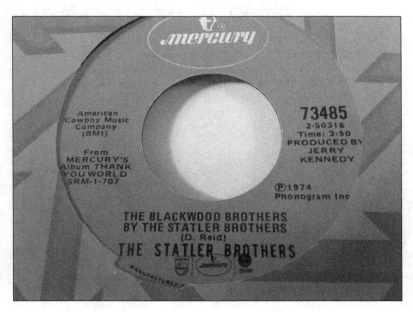

"The Blackwood Brothers by the Statler Brothers" single, written by Don Reid

11

Elvis and Voice

I had planned to leave the Blackwood Brothers at the close of the National Quartet Convention in Nashville in October of 1973. In the nearly four years since I had left the Stamps at the end of 1969, they had landed the position of singing backup for Elvis, replacing the Imperials who had begun singing with legendary entertainer, Jimmy Dean. Sometime after that, Donnie Sumner left the Stamps as well and formed a group with Sherrill Nielsen, a phenomenal tenor who had sung with the Speer Family and the Imperials, and Tim Baty, the young bass player from Michigan who had attended the Stamps School of Music in Waxahachie, Texas. They were first called The Rangers and were singing backup on the Grand Ole Opry in Nashville.

Elvis heard about Donnie's new group and contacted him about the group auditioning for Tom Jones in Las Vegas. Elvis was such a fan of gospel music I guess he thought everyone should be! He flew Donnie, Sherrill and Tim out to Vegas, had them picked up in a limo at the airport and delivered to the Hilton International where he was appearing. They auditioned for Tom there in Elvis's suite, and although Tom liked them he didn't feel there was a place for them in his show. Elvis already had the Stamps and the Sweet

Inspirations as backup singers but he offered the guys a job to just sing for him and soon developed the idea of including them in his shows in Las Vegas and on tour. In fact, he gave them an opening spot on his concerts!

That news had just hit Nashville at the time of the National Quartet Convention of 1973, which was to be my last appearance as drummer for the Blackwood Brothers. I honestly had no idea what my plans were past the convention. I just knew I couldn't stay where I was in the Blackwood Brothers Quartet. There was quite a buzz about the fact that Donnie, Sherrill and Tim were the new opening act on the Elvis Presley Show. I remember walking through the halls of the Municipal Auditorium in Nashville that night when I heard that Donnie was there and looking for me. I had traveled with him in the Stamps but wondered why on earth he wanted to talk with me. I soon found out! As an opening act on Elvis's show they needed a band, and he offered me the job of playing drums with them and I accepted it on the spot. I was on cloud nine! I remember thinking that my musical dream had come true.

I was soon met with a dissenting voice when I encountered my dad, who was also looking for me. The news that I was joining Donnie's group had gotten back to him almost immediately and he was somewhat less than thrilled with the idea. He was already very concerned about the direction my life was taking and, no doubt, grieved that I was leaving his group and stepping into a world for which I was unprepared. I was twenty years old and heading into a world that his years of wisdom told him was not the best environment for his troubled son, but there was not really much he could do to stop me. He was already resigned to the fact I was leaving the Blackwood Brothers, but this came as a real blow to him and my mother. Although their concerns are abundantly clear to me now, I was disappointed at the time that rather than being thrilled for me, they were anything but thrilled and expressed their deep concern that I was making the wrong decision. It was too late. I was up to my eyeballs in visions of grandeur. I had gone from the brink of unemployment to playing drums for an opening act on the Elvis Presley Show in a day's time.

I could write an entire book on the next two years. To quote Charles Dickens in *A Tale of Two Cities*, "It was the best of times, it was the worst of times, it was the age of wisdom, it was the age of foolishness."

Elvis changed the name of the Rangers to "Voice" and we immediately began rehearsals for our slot on stage to open his concerts. If you ever attended an Elvis concert, you understand there is really no way to describe it to someone who hasn't. He had re-emerged as a major musical icon in the Comeback Special of 1968 and had conquered Las Vegas in 1969 and the early '70s, breaking all attendance records at the Hilton International. In 1972 he played four sold out shows at Madison Square Gardens in New York City, again breaking all attendance records for a musical artist at that venue. He then became the biggest star in the history of music with "Aloha from Hawaii," the first worldwide live satellite broadcast of a concert event. Airing on January 14, 1973, it is estimated that something like one-and-a-half billion people watched the concert. It was seen by more people in the United States than the first moonwalk. The record album of the same title reached number one on the pop charts. He was playing Las Vegas and Lake Tahoe, Nevada and had resumed touring, all to sold-out venues everywhere he went.

It was the fall of that year when I joined the show. I don't know if he remembered me coming to Graceland with my dad to meet Lisa Marie, but he definitely knew whose son I was, and welcomed me to the show. We actually spent more time with him off the road than when we toured with him. In fact, in November of 1973, Donnie called and said Elvis was flying us to L.A. to come "hang out and sing." Voice was comprised of singers Donnie Sumner (J.D.'s nephew), Sherrill (Sean) Nielsen, Tim Baty, Tommy Hensley on bass guitar, Tony Brown on keyboards, John Rich on electric guitar, and myself on drums. Although I was not one of the singers, I was part of the band and I was invited/expected to be there. We boarded our chartered flight in Nashville headed for L.A. I felt like I was living in a dream. I could hardly believe this was happening.

Elvis and Priscilla had bought two homes in California, one in Beverly Hills at 144 Monovale Drive, and one in Palm Springs just off Palm Canyon Drive. I think we actually went to Palm Springs first and spent several days hanging out there. We had motel rooms in the city and would drive up to the house every day to visit. On that trip we also spent time at his home in Beverly Hills. During one of our visits there I remember riding in his white Rolls Royce driven by his stepbrother, Ricky Stanley.

One of the treasured memories of my time with Elvis happened at his home in Beverly Hills. He had created the motto TCB, with a lightning bolt, which stands for "taking care of business in a flash," and had Lowell Hays, a jewelry designer in Memphis, create a necklace with that logo. The necklaces were made of 14-karat gold and were given to members of the show and to friends. I was hanging out with Ricky Stanley in his room upstairs one night when a knock came on the door. Rick said, "Come in," and Elvis walked in with a black box. At the time I didn't know what it was but he addressed me and said, "I have something for you." He handed the box to me and I opened it. Inside was a TCB necklace. I was speechless. He took the necklace from the box and put it around my neck. I think I managed to say, "Thank you, Boss." It was official. I was really a part of the show.

You could not be around him without learning to love him. He was a giver and he loved to bless people. One such gift was a thirty-five-foot Executive motor home he bought for Voice to travel in. We were performing in some venues on our own and Elvis wanted us to have a comfortable means of travel. And comfortable it was! One such show was in Little Rock, Arkansas on February 3rd, 1975. The event was a fair buyers convention. Acts of all types would perform for these conventions in hopes of being chosen to sing at fairs across the country for the upcoming year. We had driven from our home base in Nashville a few days before, stopping in Memphis to pick up Ricky Stanley at Graceland, who was going to ride over with us.

We didn't get away from Little Rock until well after midnight when we headed for Memphis to drop Ricky off at Graceland. We then continued on Interstate 40 East towards Nashville. I had recently rededicated my life to Christ and, as the only one of the group not doing drugs, I was the designated driver. I had driven through the night after our performance and was not at the top of my game to say the least. The last thing I really remember was stopping for fuel at exit 78 in Jackson, Tennessee. The next thing I remember was driving off the side of the road at what I would later learn was mile marker 121. All the guys in the group had been asleep in various parts of the motor home as we made our way to Nashville and I had unwittingly joined them in that state of suspended consciousness.

As we crested a hill there was a drainage ditch along the side of the interstate and my right wheels became firmly settled into the rut it offered them. I had the cruise control on and upon awakening to this dilemma I was too dazed to think to simply tap the brake to disengage it. In my stupor one thing I did realize was that we were fast approaching a guardrail. In a matter of seconds we encountered it head-on.

Our back tires were churning and unknowingly plunging us toward imminent disaster. When we first hit the guard rail it was disappearing somewhere under the passenger side of the vehicle as we destroyed it in the process. Slowly but surely, though, the motor home began to drift to the right as we crested the hill and the natural slope of the road carried us that direction. I've often heard that events like this seem to happen in slow motion and this was one of those. As it became apparent we would soon be turning over on our right side every second seemed like a minute. In just a few seconds we were rolling over, and to compound the issue, a rather steep hillside had appeared just as we began our descent. We rolled over, not once, not twice, but three times as we left the interstate and tumbled helplessly down the hill, scattering pieces of the motor home and my band-mates across the hillside as we made our descent.

I have always been a seatbelt wearer. From my first days of driving as a teenager I never went anywhere without buckling up. This day was the lone exception. After I fueled in Jackson I may have already been so tired that I simply forgot. I'll never really know. What I do know is that I picked a terrible time to break my good habit. I distinctly recall that as we made that terrible first rollover I knew I had to hold on to the steering wheel or I was dead man. I grabbed that wheel and literally held on for dear life, riding the captain's chair like a bronco rider once, twice, three times over.

When we finally landed I couldn't figure out how I was still in the driver's seat clutching the steering wheel, yet there was a misty rain falling on me. We had, thankfully, landed right side up, and I remember thinking I was glad to be alive but wondering why I was in the rain. I turned to look behind me, and the entire motor home, all its contents and passengers were no longer on the chassis. All that was left on the chassis were the two captain's chairs and dashboard and steering wheel. All I could see was thirty-five feet of yellow shag carpet and nothing else. Then as I looked further back I saw the pieces of the motor home strewn across the hillside following our downward path. My first thought was that I all my band-mates were dead, perhaps in pieces strewn along with the wreckage on the rain-soaked hill down which we had just plummeted.

To my utter amazement I stared as one by one my friends began to crawl out of the debris. Sherrill had a cut on his head, Tommy a broken wrist. We would later learn that Donnie had broken his neck, the most serious of the injuries. But he was up walking as we all were trying to comprehend what had just happened. Obviously, on one level we knew what had happened, but in that first few minutes after a tragedy of this nature there is a sense of unbelief that is probably the mind's way of allowing us to process the magnitude of the event a little bit at a time. A couple of tractor-trailer drivers following behind us on the interstate had witnessed the accident. They had pulled over and raced down the wet hillside to see if they could assist us in any way. I specifically remember them saying over and over that, given the magnitude of the damage, they couldn't believe any of us made it out alive.

This was not the first time God had intervened to spare my life but it was definitely the most dramatic. And, He had not only spared my life but also the lives of my friends.

VOICE, standing, l-r, John Rich, Tony Brown, Tom Hensley, Tim Baty, seated, l-r, me, Donnie Sumner and Sherrill Neilsen

Me at the drums, circa 1974

My TCB necklace given to me by Elvis at his home in Beverly Hills making me an official member of the show, 1974

My Show Card, to be presented for access to shows and events, 1974

Elvis' Rolls Royce, now on display at Graceland, Memphis, Tennessee

12

Rededication

I joined the Elvis Presley Show with my head in the clouds and stars in my eyes. I thought I had arrived and had achieved my dream of being a drummer in a big-time show. We, for the most part, had our backgrounds in gospel quartet music but aspired to what we thought were greater heights. There are numerous clichés that come to mind, but the most appropriate may be "all that glitters is not gold." I would not be truthful if I said it wasn't fun or a thrill to be a part of the show. But I learned that although an experience is fun or thrilling, it's not worth it when you end up losing who you are in the process. The drug/party/rock 'n' roll world is a whirlwind of excitement, but devoid of reality.

Given the statistics of rock and roll celebrities who drown in unreality, it is obviously difficult to back out of it once you're in it. I think the difference for me was a combination of hearing the truth growing up in church and a Christian home and having a mom and dad and others who were praying for me. The Bible says there is pleasure in sin for a season, but when you come to the end of that season you realize where you are is not where you want to be. I certainly played the part of the prodigal son in that I left my father's home and went out into the world to a lifestyle of self-indulgence, but unlike him I didn't end up in the pig pen; just the opposite! I was eating at the "king's" table. But the wrong path is the wrong path, and being off course is the same regardless of where you land. I began to recognize I just wanted to go home.

There were a series of events that happened beginning in the fall of 1974 that God used to get my attention. The first was my being arrested for possession of a controlled substance in a church parking lot in Memphis in September. I was hanging out with a friend, smoking pot, when a patrol car drove up. I had a bag of marijuana and smoking paraphernalia with me. I was arrested and taken to jail in downtown Memphis. This was my first time in jail and I remember thinking I'd rather not spend any more time there than I absolutely had to.

I had one call and I called my brother, Jimmy. He in turn called our parents who came downtown at 3 a.m. to see me. We spoke through a small window that had three vertical bars as its main feature, probably as much for effect as actual security. I'll never forget the awkwardness and embarrassment of that conversation. When they finally turned to leave, my mom looked back through the window and said, "Remember your mama and daddy love you." It was one of those moments I can pull up in my memory and immediately return to the time and place and emotion, almost as if I were there again.

Although I can't confirm it, it was probably J.D. that told Elvis of my situation. Elvis was in very good standing with both the Memphis Police Department and the city's judicial system. When I appeared before the judge it looked like I was headed to prison for ten years for possession of a controlled substance. Everything my attorney offered, the judge quickly threw out. To say that my hearing was not going well would be an understatement. When it looked like all appeals and arguments had been to no avail and I was going to prison, the judge himself asked the arresting officer if the proper procedure for identifying the evidence against me had been duly noted at each stage of the transferring of the evidence. The officer reluctantly answered it had not. The judge immediately threw out the case against me and dismissed us from the courtroom. In less than thirty seconds I went from prison-bound to freedom.

There were members of the so-called Memphis Mafia, Elvis's bodyguards, who were with him almost constantly. One of those, Red West, was probably the closest to him. They had been friends since early on. Shortly after my courtroom drama I returned to the show for an upcoming tour. When I encountered Red, he asked me a rather strange question. He said, "Did the judge shake you up a little?" I was caught off-guard and can't recall my response but the look on his face and the tone of his voice left no doubt he knew exactly what had happened.

Many years later, another of the Memphis Mafia, Red's cousin, Sonny West and his wife, Judy, attended our church fellowship and I had the honor of being Sonny and Judy's pastor. Sonny passed away in 2017 and Judy asked if I would officiate his funeral service. Of course, I agreed and was honored to do so. Attending the funeral were many of the old Elvis entourage, most notably Red West. I was really hoping for some kind of answer to the question of what he knew about my arrest and appearance before the judge so many years ago. I mustered up the courage and walked over to him and reintroduced myself and reminded him of his question to me forty-four years earlier. He remembered me at that point and answered, "Yeah, we just told the judge you were a good kid who needed to be shaken up a bit." Ironically, that was the last time I saw Red. He died just a few months after Sonny.

I apparently didn't learn my lesson from that incident because in December of that same year, 1974, that same friend and I were on our way to Nashville to visit friends for the Christmas holidays. We had been smoking pot as we were driving. We were in my 1969

Plymouth Roadrunner. As we came into the outskirts of Nashville we took Highway 100 and turned into Percy Warner Park to cut over to south Nashville. Not long after that turn the influence of the drugs really kicked in and I ran off the road encountering one of many stone pillars that lined that scenic road through the park. I destroyed the first pillar but the second one stopped us on the spot. My friend was passed out on the front seat next to me with a gash on his lip where he had impacted the windshield.

As the police came and I sat in the back of the squad car I remember praying one of those desperation prayers like "God, if you'll get me out of this I promise I will never do this again" or some variance of that over and over for what seemed like an hour or more. And get me out of it He did. I was taken to the police station in downtown Nashville but was never booked. I honestly don't recall how the events unfolded, but I was released and that accident never even went on my record. To this day, I have no explanation except that God heard and answered my prayer. Over the next few weeks I did quit doing drugs and even the guys in Voice knew something had changed in me. The motorhome wreck just six weeks later definitely convinced me God was watching out for me and I was fortunate to be alive!

I had come to faith in Christ when I was ten years old but had walked away from that relationship in pursuit of my musical dream. Having achieved that dream, I realized I no longer wanted to live that lifestyle and, like the prodigal son, began the journey back home. That same Christmas of 1974 my dad gave me a small, leather-bound Living New Testament. I had begun to read it faithfully every night and realized more and more that the life I really wanted was something I was only going to find in Christ and nowhere else.

On April 6, 1975, the eve of my twenty-second birthday, I attended a church service at the Lord's Chapel in Brentwood, Tennessee, just south of Nashville. God met me powerfully that night and I truly felt transported to a place of absolute surrender. I honestly do not recall driving the forty-five minutes back to my home in Hendersonville after the service. The Holy Spirit was washing me in wave after wave of cleansing and renewal. I had never cried so much in my life! It was after midnight when I finally crawled into bed, emotionally exhausted but spiritually renewed. I reached to turn off my nightstand lamp and saw my little Living New Testament. I had developed the habit of reading at least a chapter in it every night and even though I was exhausted and ready to fall asleep I picked it up and began reading where I had left off the night before.

Sometime in the months preceding this event, daddy had shared with me that his favorite chapter in the Bible was 1 Corinthians 13 and he read it to me from that little Bible. Even though I had grown up in church I couldn't have told you the subject matter of that chapter or quoted any of it to you. I had read through 1 Corinthians chapter 11 the night before this renewal experience. This night I intended to read chapter 12 and go to sleep. If you are familiar with 1 Corinthians 12 you know that in it Paul talks about the gifts of the Holy Spirit but ends with the phrase, "But let me tell you about a more excellent way." Well, I wasn't about to close the book and not find out what the more excellent way was!

So, as I began to read 1 Corinthians 13 I realized this was the chapter daddy had read to me from this Bible as his favorite chapter. Well, that just turned the tears on again and I read it several more times just soaking in the great love chapter. When I finally decided I had absorbed all I could for one night I leaned up from my bed to lay the Bible on my nightstand and turn out the light. I glanced at the clock. The time was 1:03. That would be 1:03 a.m., on April 7th. I knew from the newspaper clipping my mom had saved announcing my birth that this happened to be the minute I was born twenty-two years earlier at exactly 1:03 a.m.! My birthday! At that precise moment I heard my heavenly Father say in my spirit,

"Happy birthday, son." Although I thought I had cried all I could cry, God's goodness and timing flooded me once again and I literally cried myself to sleep, with tears of absolute joy and thanksgiving.

13

Gordon Jensen and Sunrise

All I had dreamed of and worked for had proven to be far less than the pot of gold at the end of the rainbow that I had expected, and now I was looking at an uncertain future, not knowing what God had for me but knowing He was all I needed and that whatever He had for me was ultimately what I wanted. The next season was one of childlike trust in a good Father, who had proven His love for me time and time again. Ironically, God didn't impress me to leave Voice immediately. I stayed for several months after my rededication experience. In hindsight I think God was testing me to prove to Him and myself that what I had experienced was real and that the choices I had made were valid. Somewhere during the summer of that year I shared with the band that I was leaving.

Although Memphis was my hometown and Elvis's hometown, Voice was based in Hendersonville, Tennessee, twenty minutes northeast of Nashville. I had moved there in November of 1973 to join the group and be able to rehearse and participate in whatever there was to do with the position. I felt no strong inclination to move back to Memphis and I really preferred Nashville and had grown very fond of Hendersonville in particular. During the couple of years I had resided there, I became familiar with some of the recording studios and musicians and had opportunities to play on some sessions. I enjoyed those experiences tremendously and felt led to pursue those on a more regular basis. Duane Allen of the Oak Ridge Boys had a recording studio in Hendersonville and I began to play and even produce records there for gospel artists exclusively. I had known Duane from the days when they were strictly a gospel quartet and it was a natural course for me to pursue.

During my years with the Stamps and the Blackwood Brothers, we were regularly featured in concerts in the Midwest with a promoter named Lloyd Orrell. Mr. Orrell held concerts in major cities such as Detroit, Chicago, Dayton, Indianapolis, and South Bend. We played each of those cities at least once a year and sometimes twice. Lloyd's son, Larry, had a gospel group called The Orrells based in Detroit. Originally a quartet, the Orrells; Larry, Wayne Hilton and Gordon Jensen, now a trio, would often open the programs in those cities and I became a big fan of their group. Gordon wrote most of their material and played piano, Larry sang, and Wayne sang and played acoustic guitar. They had made four recordings on the Zondervan label, and then three recordings on Benson's Heart Warming label. During my two years in Voice the trio had disbanded and Wayne moved to Hendersonville to manage Duane Allen's recording studio. So, in addition to my friendship with Duane I was also well acquainted with Wayne.

Not long after Wayne moved to Hendersonville, both Larry and Gordon made the decision to leave Detroit and move there as well. Due to their great singing and the great songwriting of Gordon they had created quite a following. If you are unfamiliar with Gordon's name you may know his songs. At seventeen he wrote a song called "Redemption Draweth Nigh" that became a huge hit in the gospel music industry. "I Should Have Been Crucified," "Tears

Are a Language God Understands," "Jesus Will Outshine Them All," "Bigger Than Any Mountain," "Whisper Jesus," "He's as Close as the Mention of His Name," and "Written In Red" are some of his best known titles. After Larry and Gordon made the decision to head south there began to be some interest in the group reforming which, in fact, they did! They released a fourth record on Benson with a title song Gordon wrote called "(We're) Together Again." For reasons unknown to me, the relationship with Benson ended after that record. The Orrells had tremendous talent but really didn't fit the southern gospel concert circuit expectations. They were unique and just non-traditional enough to work their way out of a recording contract.

Not to be dissuaded, they had a brainstorming session, threw all their ideas out on the table and came up with another approach. While the name Orrells had made sense due to getting their start, singing in Larry's dad's concerts, the focus of the group had really become Gordon's songs. His songs were their calling card and identity. The decision was made to change their name to Gordon Jensen and Sunrise. Not only that, they would add to longtime bass guitarist Mark Chadwell a drummer and guitarist.

I had always admired these guys, loved their songs and their hearts, and considered them good friends, so when I was asked to join them as their drummer, I readily agreed. Mike McElravy played guitar with us for a short while and my dear lifelong friend, Stephen Speer (Ben's son), joined us playing bass guitar when Mark Chadwell decided to exit the group. Eventually, Ron Fairchild joined us playing lead guitar and keyboards. Ron's dad, Tommy, had been pianist for both the Oak Ridge Boys and the Blackwood Brothers (Ron has now been the principal keyboardist for the Oaks for thirty years). We made two records with this combination, both recorded there in Hendersonville at Duane's studio. Those records never really went very far and we certainly broke no attendance records anywhere, but the artistic satisfaction of producing our own records under the direction of Wayne Hilton was a deeply satisfying experience. One of those records was titled after Gordon's magnificent song, The Glove: "*Just an empty glove lying on the table is my life without the Master's hand. Nothing on my own, so useless alone, Lord, fill this willing glove with Your hand. Lord, let me be the glove You wear today, use me, Lord, to show someone You care today, this is all I ask as You perform your task, Lord, let me be the glove You wear.*"

This was 1976-78. The PTL Club was in its heyday and Tammy Faye Bakker fell in love with Gordon's song "Bigger Than Any Mountain." For a while we traveled to Charlotte on a monthly basis to do that song on PTL. That was about as close as we got to notoriety, not that we were in it to be famous, but it is rewarding when people appreciate what you create. On top of that, I once again had more fun than a human being should be allowed to have. These guys were great fun to share life and music with. They allowed me the opportunity to regularly share my testimony about my drift into drugs and the Elvis show and my subsequent rededication to the Lord. However, once again, the energy and effort necessary to be a viable music group proved too much to balance with the other responsibilities of life and the group disbanded. To this day I count them as some of my dearest friends. I have been on musical mission trips with both Larry to the islands of the Caribbean and with Wayne to Ecuador. Over the past couple of years we have performed a couple of Orrells reunion concerts, one at Ben Speer's Stamps-Baxter School of Music, and one at a local church in Nashville. While again significantly under the radar, these guys and those songs are among the best you'll ever hear.

When we decided to call it quits, I again looked to the Lord to help me know what He had for the next season of my life. I certainly didn't see this one coming...

Gordon Jensen & Sunrise, circa, 1976, standing, l-r, Gordon Jensen, Wayne Hilton, Larry Orrell, Mark Chadwell, seated, me

One of many appearances on the PTL Club, l-r, Jim Bakker, Wayne Hilton, Stephen Speer, Gordon Jensen, me, Larry Orrell

14

Andrus, Blackwood & Co.

My Uncle Doyle and Lavez Blackwood's first child was a son named Terry. Terry sang with the Stamps from 1962-1964, then with a group called the Memphians with his dad, Doyle, for three years. Terry was a very young man when he sang with the Stamps in the early sixties and had not really made a name for himself until he joined the Imperials in 1967.

In 1964, Jake Hess had left the Statesmen to form the Imperials, but health issues forced him to stop traveling in 1967. The Imperials had been Jake's brainchild. He wanted to have the absolute best singers in the business at his side and had certainly fulfilled that dream with Armond Morales, Sherrill Nielsen and Gary McSpadden. When his health forced him to slow his pace, he wanted the group to continue at the high level of excellence he had envisioned. Jake called my dad and asked for his input on finding a replacement for himself. My dad asked Jake if he had considered Terry. My dad knew that Terry was an excellent young singer and could do the job, and he also wanted to help his old friend. Jake took my dad's advice and hired Terry, who became known as one of the great singers in our industry.

After nine years singing with and arranging vocals for the Imperials, Terry felt it was time to move on. Sherman Andrus had originally been Andrae Crouch's lead singer in the Disciples. He had left them to join the Imperials in 1972, where he and Terry often swapped lead and baritone parts. In 1976, Sherman also felt his time with the Imperials was coming to a close. Although leaving the group a few months apart, neither Terry nor Sherman planned to start their own group. But, Word Records approached Imperials bass Armond Morales and tenor Jim Murray about leaving the Benson label and joining the Word Records family. That's exactly what happened, which left Benson without one of their premiere groups. Terry and Sherman had been the spark at the center of the Imperials, and Benson in turn approached them about forming a group for the Benson Company, and Andrus, Blackwood & Co. (AB&C) was born.

Their first record, *Grand Opening*, quickly established AB&C as a major player in the emerging contemporary gospel market. Their second record, *Following You*, built on the foundation of the first. It was just a couple of months prior to recording an album called *Live* that drummer Tim Marsh decided to leave the group. Terry and Sherman were in a bit of a pickle. They were slated to do *Live* and had no drummer. Terry called me and shared their dilemma with me, asking if I could fill in on drums for a two-week tour they were embarking on in just a few days. This was shortly after Gordon Jensen, Larry Orrell, and Wayne Hilton had decided to call it quits as a touring group. I was playing on sessions at Duane Allen's Superior Sound and wondering what the next step would be in my life and career. All Terry knew about my drumming ability was that I played. What he didn't know was that playing contemporary pop-style drums was what I did with Voice. When I filled in for those two weeks with AB&C, he and Sherman must have felt it was a pretty good fit. I ended up playing drums for them for almost seven years.

Hopefully at some point in your life you've done something or been a part of something you just felt you were made to do. It just fits like a hand in a glove and you're operating on all cylinders. That was Andrus, Blackwood & Co. for me. Shortly after I joined we recorded a *Live* concert in Evansville, Indiana. Terry and Sherman had previously recorded an acoustic version of the song, "Jesus, You're So Wonderful." On *Live,* it had great energy and it transmitted that energy to radio stations and Contemporary Christian Music (CCM) fans. It hit number one on CCM's charts in the summer of 1979 and wouldn't let go.

The guys immediately went to work on another studio record. They chose as the title song, one written by a young Nashville writer named David Baroni. The song was "Soldier of The Light." It's infectious bouncy feel and great lyric was dynamite. It exploded onto the CCM charts at #1. It was the first time in contemporary Christian music charts that a song had entered at number one. It held that spot for a year-and-a-half, and established Andrus, Blackwood & Co. as one of the top groups in CCM. For almost seven years I toured with Terry and Sherman playing the most fun music imaginable with people I loved and whose company I enjoyed.

Christian music festivals were popular during that era and we played them all, sharing the platform with Petra, Wayne Watson, Phil Keaggy, Keith Green, Twila Paris and many other CCM artists of the eighties. I realize those artists and contemporary Christian music aren't everyone's cup of tea, but for a guy like me, playing drums in that kind of band was exactly what my heart desired to do musically. During my years playing drums with the Blackwood Brothers, I was forced to play a style of music that for a teenage kid behind a drum kit was anything but fun or challenging. In AB&C everything came together. I was walking with the Lord, playing music I could help create with the talent the Lord had given me, and enjoying every last second of it.

But there was one more component of my time with AB&C I was unaware of at the time but which eventually became my greatest passion, much greater than even playing drums. Sherman Andrus had teamed up with Andrae Crouch and The Disciples in 1968 and sang with him for four years, leaving in 1972 to join the Imperials. While everyone recognized him as a great singer, at heart Sherman is a worship leader. It may have been "Jesus, You're So Wonderful" and "Soldier of The Light" that people came to concerts to see and hear performed live, but those songs just got people's attention for the main course. While the first half of our concerts was fun and uplifting, contemporary and musically cutting-edge, the second half was geared toward leading people into a worship experience. I have to tell you that in 1978 I didn't know what that even meant. I had no clue, no frame of reference for that kind of experience. Sadly, many churches talk about Jesus and teach about Him but don't understand how we can actually entertain His presence; that God, by His Spirit, actually wants to visit with His people in a tangible way whether privately or corporately.

This realization changed my life. I had no idea God was preparing me, teaching me and training me for the next phase of my life. Every concert for those six plus years I played my heart out and loved the experience, but I was really in school learning how to lead people into a worship experience using the tool of music with the Holy Spirit and Sherman as my teachers. I watched him flow with the leading of God's Spirit and gently lead the audience into a time of corporate worship like I had never experienced. As I became aware of God's presence in those concerts, I would sometimes just stop playing and get down on my knees behind the drum set, soaking in God's presence and learning how to be intimate with Him even in a public setting. Just writing about that experience takes me back to those days and I so vividly recall the feeling and the awareness of my thirst and hunger being met at a level deeper than anything I had ever known.

What I now realize is that God was pouring out His Spirit on musicians in a new and fresh way, and young worshippers, hungry and thirsty for God, were creating the dynamic we now know as praise and worship music. Whereas traditional church music had been focused on teaching theology, praise and worship choruses were giving people an expression of intimacy that wasn't wordy but worshipful nonetheless such as this simple praise song: "*I love you, Lord, and I lift my voice to worship You, O, my soul rejoice. Take joy my King in what you hear. May it be a sweet, sweet sound in your ear.*" This new kind of song sounded much like something David would have composed and sung to the Lord when he was a teenager shepherding sheep on the Judean hillsides. As Sherman Andrus led congregations and audiences in this expression of worship, I found myself being drawn to share this experience with others. When I wasn't touring with AB&C I began to lead worship with those early choruses at my own home church and God began to prepare me to walk into the next season of my life in music ministry.

Andrus, Blackwood & Co., circa, 1982, in the back, John Mays, l-r, David Ennis, Sherman Andrus, Terry Blackwood, Jeff Chambers, Randy Dennis, in front, me

Andrus, Blackwood & Co., at a Jesus Music Festival, circa 1985, l-r, Mark Burchfield, Bass player, Terry Blackwood, vocalist, me on drums, Sherman Andrus, vocalist, Jeff Chambers, guitarist.

15

The U.S. and Abroad

Many of us who were alive in the early seventies will recall the Jesus Movement. Calvary Chapel in Costa Mesa, California was the epicenter of a dramatic renewal and outpouring of God's Spirit that resulted in thousands of people coming to Christ in this sprawling part of Orange County, California. Much like the Azusa Street Revival in the early 1900s, the Jesus Movement spread like wildfire across the nation as God sovereignly poured out His Spirit on the church in a wave of revival and renewal.

In Nashville, Tennessee, an Assembly of God Church pastored by Billy Roy Moore caught the wind of this move of God. Changing their name to The Lord's Chapel, Brother Moore led the congregation into a deeper understanding of the message of grace and a freedom in worship that took the city by storm. Hundreds of people were born again, many who had dropped out of church returned to this oasis of God's presence, and the news spread. Many country music entertainers became a part of the fellowship. It was at this church where God visited me so strongly the night of my rededication to the Lord in 1975.

The youth pastor at The Lord's Chapel was a dynamic young man named Mike Nelson. Mike had a charismatic personality and a natural charm that was infectious. Coupled with a great gift of teaching God's word, the youth group grew rapidly. The Lord's Chapel was located on the south side of Nashville, the opposite side of town from where I lived in Hendersonville, but like me, people were making the forty-five-minute trek each week to be a part of what God was doing there; so many, in fact, that youth pastor Mike Nelson came to Hendersonville to the home of B.J. and Carolyn Hall to hold a Bible Study for teens. The group rapidly outgrew the Halls's home and relocated to an apartment complex clubhouse. So many teens were coming to Christ that parents became involved and many of them, too, either came to faith in Christ or renewed their commitment to Him. Thus was born the Hendersonville Chapel, holding their inaugural service the first Sunday in December 1977. I began attending in early 1978, and although my travel schedule prevented me from being there every Sunday, I loved calling it my church. Pastor Mike was as gifted a teacher and communicator as I've ever heard, and I grew much deeper in my knowledge of God and His word under his ministry.

It was November of that year that I joined Andrus, Blackwood & Co. My nearly seven years there kept me plenty busy and, as stated, I learned much from Sherman with regard to congregational worship and following the leading of the Holy Spirit. As my time with AB&C came to a close, Mike announced he was also resigning from the pastoral position at our church to begin traveling and speaking around the country. When he asked me to travel with him and lead worship before he spoke, I realized God was leading me in a new direction. Mike was a gifted speaker and Bible teacher, and his contacts around the country afforded us the opportunity to travel and minister in some wonderful locales. However, after a year of fruitful and fulfilling itinerant ministry with Mike, he developed some physical issues that demanded he cease traveling. I had left AB&C to travel with him and now found myself on my own. Looking back,

I realize God had used that year with Mike to coax me out from behind a drum kit. I had traveled as a drummer for almost two decades and had some wonderful life and ministry experiences in the process, but it was time to step out in faith into the future God had for me at that point. I had been writing songs and singing many of them in my services with Mike. Without his partnership, I began to schedule opportunities to minister, simply trusting that God was doing a work in me and that He would do one through me as well.

In 1977, I had taken a mission trip to the little island of Dominica in the West Indies with Larry Orrell, my friend and coworker from my days with Gordon Jensen. We sang there in a crusade every night for a week and saw hundreds come to faith in Christ. So, it was not surprising to me that doors began to open to travel abroad again. During the next few years I would minister in churches across the U.S. and Canada and on mission trips to Russia, England, and islands in the Caribbean.

One of the first opportunities I had to minister as a worship leader was with my dear friend, Denny Duron. Denny pastors in Shreveport, Louisiana and was also instrumental in the foundation and organization of Athletes International Ministries (AIM), a conference designed to reach athletes for Christ. Denny had played football professionally for a short while but chose to leave that world to return to his alma mater and coach football for his college team. Having made many friends in the sports world, he joined with two of his friends to create AIM. Hundreds of athletes and their spouses attended. There were many professional athletes and coaches of the day who answered the call to partner with Denny, his friend, Larry Kerychuk, and Ed Mooney to host annual conferences in Phoenix to reach young and old collegiate and professional athletes for the kingdom of God. Helping to lead worship, I had the privilege of being a part of a few of those conferences during the late 1980s. In attendance were Dallas Cowboys coach Tom Landry,

University of Colorado coach Bill McCartney, players A.C. Green of the Lakers, Mike Singletary of the Chicago Bears, Reggie White of the University of Tennessee and Green Bay Packers, Meadowlark Lemon of the Harlem Globetrotters, and many, many more. It was at one of those conferences that God gave Colorado coach Bill McCartney the vision for Promise Keepers. I saw Craig Morton, former quarterback for the Dallas Cowboys, New York Giants and the Denver Broncos, stand at the podium and weep in the presence of the Lord. Hundreds of athletes, both collegiate and professional, came to faith in Christ at those conferences. It was an awesome time and I was so grateful for the experience.

In 1989 my dad called and said he had been invited to be a part of a team traveling to Russia. He wondered if I would be interested in going with him. I jumped at the chance! Going to Russia with my dad? Of course! Part of our mission was to smuggle Bibles into the country. Every member of the team had two suitcases; one with personal effects and one loaded with Russian Bibles! Our cover was that my dad and I were scheduled to sing in churches as part of a cultural exchange program. On that trip we visited Moscow and Leningrad (which has now regained its original name, St. Petersburg), and Kiev, Ukraine. We flew from Memphis to New York City to London and then on to Moscow for the first stop on our trip.

While we were there we had one of the most memorable experiences of my life. We were scheduled to sing at First Baptist Church in Moscow on a cold Sunday morning in January of 1990. The church building was a huge grey stone structure that was cavernous in appearance. There were places in the ceiling where daylight shone through, perhaps a result of bombings during the war. The place was packed. I can still see that sea of precious Russian believers standing shoulder to shoulder, dressed in their wool topcoats, scarves and hats, as it was just about as cold inside as out. Because of the language barrier, we spoke through an interpreter.

So many years later, some of the details of that morning escape me, but one thing etched in my memory is my dad and I singing "How Great Thou Art." He sang a verse and a chorus and I sang a verse and chorus. Each time we started the chorus, the congregation, obviously familiar with the song, joined in, singing it in their native Russian language. As I write these words, my eyes well up with tears. I am transported back to that sanctuary on that frigid January morning and I can see them and hear them singing. I was changed that morning. My view of God, His love for mankind and His ability to reach and touch people regardless of political or ideological differences lodged firmly in my consciousness.

Our trip to Leningrad and Kiev were also life-changing, memorable experiences. We met many brothers and sisters in Christ, most of whom we would never have known and whom we will likely never see again until heaven. They were so appreciative that we came. We sang in each of the cities in a host church and were guests at a meal in each place. We never saw our suitcases with Bibles once we arrived in each city. I'm sure it was prearranged to have those suitcases taken to a safe place upon our arrival. I also developed a new appreciation for how precious God's Word is. When you witness people willing to risk everything to get God's Word, you realize how dear it is.

I had the privilege of visiting the UK on three occasions during that period. My first trip, in 1989, allowed me to minister not only in churches, but in schools as well. At that time in England, public schools had Religious Education classes. Guests were welcome to present their religious view as long as it was done respectfully and not overtly proselytizing. My being from the United States and my association with Elvis gave me a platform to share my faith in the context of my musical experiences. I returned in 1990 and 1991, staying six weeks in '91, ministering not only in England, but in Wales and on the island of Guernsey. To say I fell in love with the

British people would not be an exaggeration. I made friends there who keep in touch to this day. I also made a second trip to Russia in 1990, again ministering in the same three cities and carrying suitcases of Bibles into the country. This trip was without my dad and I was afforded the opportunity to preach in Leningrad with our friend, Rev. Sergei Nikolai. Pastor Nikolai had been to the U.S. and had even traveled for a short while with the Blackwood Brothers to raise money for Bibles to Russia. It was an honor to preach in his church with him interpreting my message.

While the travel and thrill of meeting people from other countries and sharing our mutual love of Christ was exhilarating, I began to sense a deep desire to settle down and focus my attention on my local church. Little did I know that the next few years would be some of the most challenging yet rewarding of my life.

Hendersonville Chapel founding pastor, Mike Nelson, and me, circa 1986

My first overseas mission trip to Dominica, W. I. with Larry Orrell. 1987

Me at the piano leading worship in Dominica, 1987

Daddy and me in Red Square, Moscow, Russia, January 1990

16

The Hendersonville Chapel

BY THE EARLY 1990S I FELT THE LORD LEADING me to really put my roots in deep and focus on whatever ministry He would have me to do at home. I approached my pastor, who had been mentored by Mike Nelson, and told him what I felt the Lord speaking to me. He expressed that there was definitely a place for my gifts there, and in April 1993 I went on staff full-time at the Hendersonville Chapel. I served as the youth pastor and led musical worship for both the youth and adult services. At the time, about 500 people attended the church on Sunday mornings. Being a member there for fifteen years prior to going on staff, I was very acquainted with the body of believers, and our lives were already woven together in deep, meaningful relationship. The Chapel was a unique place, focused much more on preaching the word, on building the kingdom and trusting God to bring the increase, and less on denominational ties and traditions. It had grown to 1,200 people at its peak when Mike stepped down, and although it had gone through a refining process by the time Pastor John McLendon came, it was still a strong, vibrant body of believers.

As I stepped into the roles of pastoring the youth and leading worship for both the youth and adult services, I found myself in a season of tremendous blessing. God was pouring into the lives of students, and worship was deep and intimate. One of the things God did during that season was to put me in fellowship with other youth ministers in the city. The youth pastors at two large Baptist churches, the United Methodist Church, the Church of Christ and others began to meet at least once a quarter and pray together for each other, for the youth of our city and for God to send revival. Out of that group grew some close friendships. As we met and prayed, God knit our hearts together and we saw ourselves as all serving on the staff of the same church with a common goal to reach the youth of our city and to trust the Lord to funnel them wherever He saw fit. One of the Baptist youth pastors and I began to lead worship at the Fellowship of Christian Athletes meetings on Friday mornings at the local high school. It grew till the band room where we met was filled to overflowing every Friday as a couple hundred students came together to worship before school began.

On several occasions we held citywide youth events, bringing all our students together to meet in what is now the TBN theatre in Hendersonville, Tennessee. Our gathering began to draw the attention of contemporary Christian artists. During the middle nineties, Amy Grant released a record of youth worship songs that were sung at a youth meeting held regularly in the barn on her property. The project was called *Songs from The Loft*. Many youth groups around the country had incorporated these songs into their worship repertoire, as had we. Somehow word got to her about our youth meetings in Hendersonville and one night she and her husband, Gary Chapman, came with a full band to lead several of those songs for the seven hundred or so teenagers in the house. No charge, no publicity, just a desire to come and bless what God was doing. Over the next few years the interest in getting together unfortunately waned, some leaders moved on, and we never regained that unity, but while it lasted it was a taste of heaven, the body being one, at least at the youth level.

Worship at the Chapel continued to grow and excel. I had heard about a revival in Pensacola, Florida where God was doing some pretty interesting things. I decided to go check it out for myself. I sensed a powerful movement of God during my three days there and came back with a renewed passion for ministry. The rest of the staff apparently saw fruit that made them desire to experience what I had experienced, so our entire staff and spouses attended a pastoral conference there in Pensacola the next year. About that time, we were asked by a sister congregation in the city if they could use our facility for a revival. They were going to host it but felt their building wouldn't accommodate the anticipated crowd and we agreed to let them use our building.

The revival was scheduled for a couple of weeks in March of 1999, but God had other plans. Five nights a week and twelve weeks later it finally concluded. God moved in miraculous ways and many were brought into the kingdom. Many people who attended were from backgrounds that had never seen a church service that was not scripted and typed in a bulletin. The freedom of worship and the spontaneous words of testimony and exhortation were new territory for some, but for all who attended there was agreement that God was up to something. Our normal Sunday morning church services became anything but. I recall one Sunday morning when one of our most conservative, staid elders stood at the podium and wept openly and testified of how controlling he had been and that he was learning to trust God to lead our congregation. That was a season of tremendous hope and promise.

During the revival, a guest speaker who really didn't know me called me up in front of the congregation one night. I had been standing in the sound booth making sure all the technical needs of the moment were addressed. I was very surprised when he called me by name and asked me to come forward. I walked to the front of the sanctuary and stood there facing him as he began to share. He said that sometimes God reveals things to you you can't know any other way than that He simply shares them with you. You may not know a person or a situation but God, by his Spirit, reveals things about a person or situation and, in so doing, verifies He is the One directing what is being said. In scripture it is called a word of knowledge and is a gift of the Holy Spirit listed in 1 Corinthians chapter 12. This gentleman began to share how, as he was praying before the service that night, God began to reveal things to him about me. What he couldn't have known was my role at that church. I had been the youth pastor and worship leader for several years, but as of 1999 our church had been without a senior pastor and I had taken on some of the responsibilities of a senior pastor by default. During that year our church had continued to grow numerically and financially, and I was just doing my best to hear from God and follow His leading, not sure where it was all headed.

All that changed that night. As I stood before him, the intensity of his voice increased and he began to speak over me that I had been like a utility player on a ball team (for those unfamiliar with the term, a utility player on a team does a lot of things, filling whichever role needs to be filled and playing whichever position is vacant). He said God was getting ready to take me into a new season of ministry and that He was placing an anointing on me for leadership. There is no way this man could have known what God had been speaking to my heart. I had shared it with no one at that point. I began to weep as he kept talking and declaring what God was revealing to him. I eventually went to my knees. Why God chose this way to convince me of what He was calling me to I don't know, but I know He was confirming it just as Moses knew. I got up from my knees that night totally undone, wondering what it all meant.

17

FATHERS DAY

1999 WAS A PIVOTAL YEAR FOR THE CHAPEL AND for my family and me. On Father's Day that year I was scheduled to preach. I had been studying the role of fathers in the ancient Jewish family and I felt God gave me an idea. In my studies I had read a book called The *Ancient Paths* by Craig Hill. The point of the book was revealing that in traditional Old Testament Jewish families the father would speak blessing over his children on a regular basis but particularly at certain times, most notably at a Bar Mitzvah, when a son turned thirteen. He would anoint his son with oil and speak God's blessing over him. In a nutshell, the Ancient Paths states that traditional Jewish fathers gave their children a sense of identity (who they were) and a sense of destiny (where they were going). I felt God instructed me to have each head of household, whether dad or mom, anoint their children and pray blessing over them.

We found a supplier for little glass vials and I filled them all with oil, knowing we would have a couple hundred families there that morning. We made sure each head of household had a vial and I shared that in the traditional Jewish family the dads would anoint their children and pray blessing over them, declaring their value and worth and speaking God's destiny over them. After the message concluded, we had the family units gather together and I wrote a prayer and blessing for the parents to speak over their children and instructed them to anoint their children with a drop of oil on their head much as the Jewish fathers of thousands of years ago would have done.

This is the conclusion of the sermon and the prayer we prayed on Father's Day, 1999: "The Word of God says that Abraham blessed Isaac, and Isaac blessed Jacob. Malachi 4:6 says, 'I will turn the hearts of the Fathers toward their children, and the children to their mothers/fathers.' James 5:16 says, 'Confess your sins one to another that you may be healed.' What we are about to do is be obedient to God's Word."

Fathers, I want you to face your children; children, face your father. Fathers, repeat after me: "My precious child, I love you. The seed that became your life was placed in me by God. He chose you to be my child and me to be your father. I am incapable of loving you perfectly, although that is the desire of my heart. In some ways I have passed on to you the imperfections passed on to me from my parents. I confess as sin those times when I have disciplined you in anger and not in love, and I ask your forgiveness. I confess as sin those times I have placed my career, or my desire for things, or the pursuit of pleasure above loving you. Please forgive me. Those times do not accurately reflect the love I have for you. As a child of God, created in His image, my love for you goes deeper than I can express, just as His love for us as His children goes deeper than we can comprehend. With the help of God, empowered by His Holy Spirit who lives within me, I will from this day forward seek to be a godly father, a man of integrity, realizing that loving God, and knowing Him, is my greatest need, and that modeling, exampling, and reflecting His love to you, is my highest calling as your father. Please be patient with me. I'm not perfect and at times I will fail to love you perfectly, but I will always love you. Remember that I am being perfected and conformed to the image of Christ Jesus just as you are."

Mothers, face your children; children, face your mothers. Mothers, repeat after me: "My precious child, I love you. God knit you together in my womb. He chose you to be my child, and me to be your mother. I am incapable of loving you perfectly, although that is the desire of my heart. In some ways I have passed on to you the imperfections passed on to me from my parents. I confess as sin those times when I have disciplined you in anger and not in love, and I ask your forgiveness. I confess as sin those times I have placed my career, or my desire for things, or the pursuit of or pleasure above loving you. Please forgive me. Those times do not accurately reflect the love I have for you. As a child of God, created in His image, my love for you goes deeper that I can express, just as His love for us as His children goes deeper than we can comprehend. With the help of God, empowered by His Holy Spirit who lives within me, I will from this day forward seek to be a godly mother, a woman of integrity, realizing that loving God, and knowing Him, is my greatest need, and that modeling, exampling, and reflecting His love to you, is my highest calling as your mother. Please be patient with me. I'm not perfect and at times I will fail to love you perfectly, but I will always love you. Remember that I am being perfected and conformed to the image of Christ Jesus just as you are."

Parents, please place your hand on your child's head and repeat after me: "My precious child, I receive you as God's gift to me. Whatever the circumstances regarding your conception you are God's gift to me and I treasure you. I bless you in the name of the Lord. I pray you will come to know and continue to grow in the love of God. I pray you will have a hatred for sin. I pray you will be protected from the evil one in every area of your life; spiritually, physically, and emotionally. I pray you will choose friends who will lead you toward God and not away from Him. I pray you will respect those in authority over you even when they are wrong. I pray you will be kept from the wrong kind of mate and saved for the right kind of mate. I pray that from this day forward you will be kept sexually pure until the day you marry. I pray you will totally submit to God and resist the enemy. I plead the blood of Jesus over your life to cover you, to cleanse you, to keep you, and the person of the Holy Spirit to fill you, to guide you, and to empower you, to be everything God has created and called you to be. I pray that God would release right now a vision of your destiny in Him and the service to which He has called you. In Jesus's name, Amen."

Okay, guys and girls, it's your turn. Face your parent(s) and repeat after me. Whichever applies, say, "Dear mom/dad, I love you. As I become an adult it is hard for me to break away from you. Part of me wants to and part of me wants to hold you forever. But as long as I am in your care and under your roof I submit to your God-given authority over me! Forgive me for the times I've been disobedient, disrespectful, unkind, and unloving. I do love you. I realize that as I submit to you I am submitting to God. His Word commands me to honor my father and my mother, whether you are right or wrong, having a good day or a bad day. Forgive me for being self-centered, focused on what my needs are and how to meet them. Be patient with me. Remember that I am being perfected and conformed to the image of Jesus just as you are."

Parents, please respond, "I love you and I forgive you."

Parents, please take the vial of oil you have, open it, place your index finger over the opening and turn it to allow a drop of oil to rest on your finger. Now make the sign of the cross on the forehead of your child and repeat after me:

"I anoint you in the name of our Lord Jesus Christ to be everything He has created and destined you to be and to receive everything He desires you to receive. This oil is a type or symbol of the Holy Spirit and right now I pray for the infilling and empowering of the Holy Spirit of Almighty God to fill you and flood your life. He will lead you into all truth and will reveal God's will to you as you submit daily to His leading. In Jesus's name. Amen."

What made this morning extra special for me personally was that my mom and dad were visiting us and were in the service. At the conclusion my dad came forward and I handed him a vial of oil and asked him to bless me. He anointed me and prayed a beautiful prayer over me.

I have been around long enough to know that you may be reading this and thinking this is way out of your comfort zone. It was something I had never seen but again, I was simply trying to hear from God and obey what I heard. On occasion, people still mention that day to me. It was life-changing for some families and for our church family. Some people claim God no longer speaks to us and that everything He had to say is in His written Word. But in John chapter 10, Jesus says that His sheep know His voice. I have certainly witnessed people claiming to hear from God and then doing things that contradict the Bible. Anything God impresses us to do will never contradict His word, but to claim He no longer speaks to us seems unscriptural and unrealistic to me. I think it's possible that in order to not have to deal with those who claim they hear from God but clearly don't, some people would rather claim God no longer speaks to His children. That may solve the problem of having to deal with people who are in error, but it also has the unintended consequence of failing to hear when God wants to say something to us. I guess I just can't accept that a loving Father never speaks to His children. When I read God's Word I certainly feel at times that scripture is speaking to me, and there are times when I'm simply in prayer and God impresses me with something that blesses me or blesses others, which is the effect my Father's Day message had that day.

18

Daddy & Mama

Obviously, I would not be here if not for my parents, and up to this point I have not really focused on the role my dad and mom played in my life. Many people knew my dad because of his involvement in gospel music and his leadership in the Blackwood Brothers. Although he was the youngest of the three brothers in the original group, his brothers, Roy and Doyle, retired from the group in the late 1940s, leaving my dad and his nephew, R.W. as the only Blackwoods in the group. Daddy assumed the leadership of the group at that point and continued in that position until the early 1980s when he left to form the Masters V with J.D. Sumner, Hovie Lister, Jake Hess and Rosie Rozelle.

I could sum up my dad with this cliché: *To know him was to love him*, and literally thousands did. Daddy not only possessed a tremendous voice, but an even greater heart. I've already shared how poor he was as a kid, but rather than become greedy when he became successful, he gave and gave and gave. Both he and my mom were generous to a fault. He loved people and people loved him back. He also had an amazing memory for names. I can't tell you how many times someone has told me they met my dad once, saw him years later and he called them by name! And it didn't matter if you were the President or the janitor, he had time to talk and loved to do so.

His accolades are many. There is a wall in my and dad's home literally covered with awards and honors: seven Gospel Music Association Dove Awards as the Best Male Vocalist in gospel music, nine Grammy's for Best Gospel Performance, keys to cities, plaques, and on and on. I firmly believe it was not just daddy's talent that earned him those awards; it was his connection with people. People knew daddy was real and that he genuinely loved the Lord and people. Don't get me wrong, he wasn't perfect. He had flaws and faults like every other human being, but he had a heart for God and a heart to be used of God. That was the James Blackwood the audiences and fans knew.

Then there was daddy at home. My mom said he would play with us as long as we'd play. He absolutely loved being a dad and it showed. Mama said that one night as I was a baby not wanting to go to sleep, daddy was walking up and down the hall holding me in his arms trying to get me to go to sleep and rocking me as he walked. He commented to my mom that if having children wasn't so hard for her he'd want "one of these" a year.

Traveling as a kid with my dad was a huge treat. I saw much of the world because of his talent and popularity. As I mentioned in chapter nine, the Blackwood Brothers took an eighteen-day tour of the capitals of Europe and the Holy Land in the Summer of 1968. We crisscrossed Europe and ended the tour with six days in Israel. My mom and I accompanied my dad, the group and approximately forty-five close friends and fans on that life-changing trip. And I accompanied him to Russia and the Ukraine in 1989, but it was the trips as a kid that really entertained me, traveling on the bus, seeing different cities. His was not the typical job and, as a result, mine was not the typical childhood.

The advantage of his travel was also a disadvantage. Most any child with a dad in a profession that included travel can attest how you look forward with great anticipation to dad coming home or, if you had really misbehaved, you dreaded seeing him walk through the door. My childhood was pretty much split down the middle with regard to the anticipation/dread scale. My mom was the consummate homemaker and mother. She worked as hard as daddy did, but her energies were directed at keeping the home fires burning, and raising my brother, Jimmy, and me. Jimmy is almost ten years my senior and it's obvious my parents hadn't much practice when it came to raising him. By the time I came along they had learned from their mistakes, which is why I turned out so much better than he did. (You realize I'm kidding, right?)

My one claim to fame as a kid is that I could run pretty fast. I recall my mom and dad coming to school on "field days" to watch me run. There were only a couple other guys in my elementary school who were any competition, and one of the three of us always won the races. Having always had a somewhat diminutive stature, being able to run fast served me well in more ways than on the playing field. Bigger bullies liked to practice their craft on guys like me, and more than once I survived by being able to run faster than they could. Apparently, I was also the kid in a restaurant or a store that caused the other adults to look at my dad and mom and me and think to themselves, "Can't you do anything with that kid?" To deal with me in those situations, my mom had a harness for me. It was the only thing that kept me from disappearing anytime we went somewhere. It wasn't long, however, before I figured out that by grabbing a pole or some other stationary object, she would then remove the harness at which point I'd take off.

There were a few times she also came to my rescue. One such time I had ridden my bike several blocks from home. As I began the journey home after dark, a man was walking down the street approaching from the opposite direction. He crossed over to my side of the road just a house or two ahead of me. It could have been that he meant no harm but I was scared. At just that moment my mom came driving up in our family car. She quickly opened the trunk, I threw my bike in and off we went before there was any opportunity for interaction. She later told me that she felt a strong urge to stop what she was doing and to come check on me. We have talked about that incident through the years and both have concluded that the Holy Spirit prompted her to come to my rescue!

During my drug use years, my mom and dad prayed and struggled to keep the lines of communication open between us. I was an adult out on my own and, as such, out from under their supervision and protection, but not out from under the power of their prayers and their love for me as their child. My dad was still traveling with the Blackwood Brothers at the time. Someone pitched him a song called "A Father's Prayer," which he recorded and which became the title of a long play record. It was obvious from the lyric he had me in mind when he sang it. "Give my child one more chance to pray" was part of the lyric. All these years later with kids, and now grandkids of my own, I realize the heartache of having a child go through times of rebellion and walking away from the things of God. Fortunately, in my life and the lives of my children, those times of rebellion were followed by repentance and turning back to the Lord. As I've often told my children, "Your decisions determine your destiny." When those decisions and choices are guided by God's Word, His Holy Spirit and the counsel of godly friends and advisors, it makes for a much better life. Can I get an *'amen'*?

Daddy passed away on February 3, 2002, at eighty-two years of age. Family, fans and friends numbering approximately 2,000 filled our home church to honor him. Paul Harvey acknowledged his passing on his daily radio program. Daddy died on a Sunday. I suppose I would remember it well in any case, but it happened to be as

I was preaching. We knew he was not long for this world and I was wearing a pager knowing his passing was imminent. I was reaching the conclusion of the message that day when my pager went off, not once or twice but several times. It was difficult to keep my train of thought knowing the message that awaited me was the death of my dad.

My mom passed away in 2019 at the ripe old age of ninety-seven and was able to stay in her home until just a few months before she died. My brother, Jimmy and sister-in-law, Mona, made countless trips to her house to make sure her needs were met, and when it became apparent she was no longer able to stay by herself they moved her into their home. For many people with aging parents, one of the saddest transitions in life is seeing them, or worse yet, having to choose for them to leave their home. Daddy made sure mama would be taken care of financially, and Jimmy and Mona took on the responsibility of taking care of her as her health declined. There will be stars in their crowns for how they took care of her in her last days.

My only sibling, Jimmy, has been married to his high school sweetheart, Mona, for fifty-six years as of 2019. I barely remember life without Mona. She has been much more like a sister to me and a daughter to my mom and dad. Jimmy sang in the Blackwood Brothers from 1970-1986, at which time he went into full-time solo ministry. You may not know that Jimmy was healed of pancreatic cancer in 1984. He was weak, jaundiced, and had been given three to six weeks to live. While awaiting surgery the doctor ran tests, which contradicted earlier tests showing the mass on his pancreas. So, the original tests were rerun and no mass was found. His recovery was extremely rapid and he resumed travel immediately. As the testimony of his healing became more widely known, he left the Blackwood Brothers to pursue a solo ministry, returning to the Blackwood Brothers again in the early 2000s, finally retiring from the group in 2012.

Mama & Daddy

Our family, circa, 1958, clockwise from left, My mom, my dad, my brother, Jimmy, and me

Our family in Birmingham, AL, circa, 1989, l-r, me, daddy, mama, Jimmy

My mom and dad with President Jimmy Carter, Washington, D.C., circa 1978

My mom and dad and I on a cruise with Dr. Charles Stanley, 1988

My mom and dad with Mr. & Mrs. Albert E. Brumley, circa 1970

My mom and dad with First Lady, Barbara Bush, 1991

My mom and dad with dear friends, Brock & Faye Speer, 1998

My mom and dad with dear friends, Jake & Joyce Hess, 1998

My mom and dad, 1999

19

No-Mader What

"'I KNOW THE PLANS I HAVE FOR YOU,' SAYS THE Lord; 'plans to give you a hope and a future'" (Jer. 29:11). God is omniscient, a fancy word that means He knows everything, every thought, every word, every action of every creature on earth from the beginning till the end of time and reaching to eternity past and future. As such He knows the intimate details of our lives, our attitudes, our emotions, the thought processes behind every thought we think, and every action we take or fail to take, whether pure or impure, noble or ignoble. But God has plans for us that are only good! Romans 8:28 says, *"...all things work together for good to those who love God, to those who are the called according to His purpose."* God is also under no obligation to reveal His plans to us. Someone once said that if we knew all the future held we'd probably faint, overwhelmed by the magnitude of that knowledge. God knew we could only handle life one day at a time and He created us to do just that. And no matter what happens, we can trust God, even when we feel like a nomad!

I don't know if you have ever been in a place or time where you knew God was revealing something to you only to watch as others failed to see it. In the months following the revival at our church during the summer of '99, some who had been on board retreated to the safety and familiarity of the way things used to be. It reminded me of how Peter responded in Antioch when James's disciples came from Jerusalem. Peter, who had fully bought into grace and freedom from keeping the law, began to withdraw from Paul and the converts there. Paul rebuked him in a powerful passage of scripture found in Galatians chapter 2. In the months that followed revival, decisions were made that completely quenched the Holy Spirit. I felt deeply that God had a word of rebuke for the leadership or our church, and although I pleaded with the Lord to choose anyone but me to deliver it, He would not relent.

One of the analogies the Lord had given me to share was that we were standing on the edge of the Promised Land and we allowed the negative testimony of a few to send fear through the leadership. As God is my witness, I would have rather skipped that meeting. I argued with God, but by then I knew what I had to do. Many times I had read where God inspired Old Testament prophets to deliver a word no one wanted to hear. Never in my wildest dreams did I think God would have me do something like that. Two precious men of God and brothers stood with me as I delivered it with tears. It was not well received. Within six months I resigned my position and left the church body I loved. This began a year of nomadic wandering, visiting local churches, trying to find a home and ministering whenever and wherever God opened the door.

When I resigned my position at the Hendersonville Chapel, I didn't know what God's plans were; I just knew what they weren't. When I had traveled in itinerant music ministry in the late 1980s and early 1990s, I had felt God instructed me to never set a fee for ministry but to trust Him to meet my needs. I did, however, call churches and pastors in pursuit of places to minister. I had spent the last seven years on staff at a church and was now without employment. My natural inclination was to go back to what I had always done, which was traveling. That seemed to be the direction God was leading me, but He impressed upon me that this time not only should I never set a fee, but I should also not call to schedule services! He would open the doors He wanted me to walk through. I have to tell you, that was a leap of faith! No income, now married with three little girls and a fourth on the way, and I was just supposed to trust that God would provide.

Well, provide He did! People began to send money—sometimes sizable amounts to support us. It was absolutely amazing. And churches called and scheduled me to come sing and share my testimony and God poured resources into our ministry. It was a faith walk, but God proved Himself faith*ful!* For the entire year of 2000 we simply trusted God, walked through the doors He opened and received His provision. We visited several churches in the area but nothing felt like a good fit. Many of our close friends had left our former church for the same reasons we did and we were like a bunch of wandering nomads. Twenty-five or thirty of us would often gather at the home of one particular couple and have great fellowship, eating and worshipping together.

Over the course of that year God began to do something radical in my heart. I began to sense Him calling me to start a church fellowship. If you are surprised at that thought, let me tell you no one was more surprised than I was! The home group with whom we were meeting was almost exclusively people who had attended our former church. I had been on staff there as the worship pastor for seven years and many of these precious friends began to sense we were to begin a new work. In hindsight it really wasn't a radical idea. When something is healthy it produces new life. I just couldn't wrap my mind around being the one to lead it. Although I had never been to seminary, I had received an ordination certificate from our church for the years I had spent in ministry and the courses I had taken. But still, pastoring? Have you ever read the story of Moses and how he argued with God about leading the nation of Israel? Well, that was me. I argued with God for months. All the while, we kept visiting area churches but nothing felt like home.

The clincher came one day in Indianapolis. I was there for a Gaither video recording. My dad was there as well and we had lunch together on day two of the taping. As I was sitting across the table from him I mustered the courage to share with him how I felt like God was calling me to pastor. I honestly expected him to laugh or give me a stern reply that I wasn't equipped for such a position. His reply nearly stopped my heart. He said, "Your mother and I have been praying about that." I was completely floored. That was the moment I knew what I was sensing really was from God and that a new chapter of ministry was about to open that would take me places I had never dreamed. As we sat and shared, daddy encouraged me to hear from God and obey what I heard regardless of what anyone thought or said. His counsel to me that day helped solidify the direction God was giving me and proved to be an invaluable piece of advice that confirmed what God was telling me.

In the years since that day I have often thought of how God used my sweet daddy to speak into my life. He was not someone who would have shared his thoughts lightly. It was obvious to me he was deeply sincere and as aware as I was of the magnitude of what God was calling me to do. Praise God for godly parents!

Gateway

During the year of 2000 I had been serving on a volunteer basis at a small local church and many of our fellow Chapel family migrated there. In my desire to be part of a local body of believers I had jumped in with both feet and served wherever I could. These were precious people, many of them already friends of ours, but some new faces as well. For that year after the Chapel God loved me and my family through that precious congregation and, although I gave it everything I had and truly sought to be a part of that church body, God had other plans I could neither ignore nor evade. God, by His Spirit, was calling me to serve as a lead pastor and I was arguing with God and doing all I knew to do to convince myself I wasn't qualified or educated for that position. Then came the lunch with my dad at the Gaither taping and I realized that God was not the one mistaken, and that I was to start a new work for the group of friends who were looking for leadership and a fresh start.

On New Year's Eve 2000 we hosted a gathering of like-minded believers in a small storefront in Hendersonville, Tennessee. I really didn't know what to expect. I just had an unmistakable sense God was leading us, and our part was to hear as best we could and follow as closely as we could follow. About forty or fifty of our friends joined us for a night of worship. I can't tell you a song we sang or a word I preached or even if I preached. I think we shared communion and we prayed and sang and enjoyed the fellowship of the believers.

In January of 2001 I woke up early one morning before the sun was up with a feeling God wanted to share something with me. I made my way to my prayer chair and sat with my laptop and my Bible waiting for what might come next. The Holy Spirit directed me to draw a cross, which I did. He then began to download something to me that I had never heard, but it seemed as if what He was sharing with me was foundational. I began to write... The cross—it's all about relationship. The Holy Spirit kept speaking and I continued to write until about thirty minutes later I had the sense I had received what God had for me. That download became the foundation of our church fellowship. I knew God was giving me a life message and that it would be the core of what I was to share with people.

Here is the download and the way I sensed God led me to present it:

The Cross— It's All About Relationship

"The Cross is the symbol of Christianity for obvious reasons, but also for some 'not-so-obvious' reasons. The obvious reason is the fact that Jesus was crucified on the Romans' instrument of choice for inflicting the greatest pain and humiliation inhumanly possible. One of the not-so-obvious reasons is the fact that the cross represents a dynamic of Christianity only understood by those for whom the cross has become their identity. That dynamic is *relationship.*

The cross is comprised of two beams—one vertical and one horizontal. The vertical beam represents our relationship to God.

The horizontal beam represents our relationship to others in the human family. The horizontal beam is wholly dependent upon the vertical beam to maintain its place. Without the vertical beam it is impossible for the horizontal beam to function.

That's the way it is in the 'family' of Christianity. Our relationship with God is the basis for our relationship with each other. Only as we are in right relationship with our Father can we hope to be in right relationship with others. Christianity is all about *relationship*; first with our Creator, and then and only then, with His creation.

Jesus, God's Son, came from the Father, not to establish a religion but to restore a relationship; relationship that was broken by sin, which is man's disobedience to God's moral law. Through His obedience we have the opportunity to be in right relationship to our Creator, God, and in right relationship with our human family.

God, by His Spirit, lives in everyone who places their faith in Jesus, and as we submit to the work of His Spirit He gives us the ability to love, to serve, and to give in ways that would never be possible in our own power. Although no one will ever walk through this life perfectly like Jesus, we know that His Spirit is changing us and empowering us to be like Him."

I will certainly never be called a theologian and I can't claim that I somehow came up with this insight. God simply put it in my heart and mind and I took dictation as He did so. In the years that have followed that revelation, I have come to believe it even more deeply than the day I first received it.

Thinking we should have a name for our church, I decided on a name drawn from two scriptures. In John chapter 10, verses 7 and 9, Jesus calls Himself the Door (some translations read 'Gate') and in

John 14:6 He calls Himself the Way, the Truth, and the Life. I settled on two of those metaphors, Gate and Way, and we named our fellowship GateWay. I grew up in church but I had never heard the emphasis on relationship that God seemed to be spotlighting, and if you asked anyone in our church what GateWay was about, they would have quickly told you, *relationship*. It was a clear, simple, biblical concept that, as I said, became the foundation of our fellowship. We not only met corporately on Sundays and Wednesdays, but also in small home groups throughout the week where smaller groups could develop greater intimacy and accountability.

Our first Sunday was on April 1st, 2001. That first service we had about sixty people. I preached from John chapter 10 about Jesus being the Good Shepherd and how we could expect to hear His voice. I was so amazed by all that was happening, and I kept expecting to wake up from a dream. But God was so gracious to me, and what I lacked in formal education, He seemed to make up for in other ways. We outgrew our first little meeting place almost immediately. Seventy-five people was about all we could squeeze in. And squeeze we did! We were blest with an abundance of great musicians for our worship team, and with a great cross-section of believers who helped activate and facilitate the work of the ministry.

After a couple of months of looking for a larger place of worship, we found a new home in the neighboring town of Goodlettsville, Tennessee. This one would easily hold three times the people we had and gave us room for growth. And it just kept growing and growing. Two years later, on Easter Sunday 2003, we had 300 people in attendance that day. The place was wall-to-wall people and we used every chair we could find to give everyone a seat. GateWay was like a bumble bee. You know that, aerodynamically speaking, they're not supposed to be able to fly, but fly we did! It was also like a hospital, where people who were spiritually sick could come and get healed and set free. And it was like a family. Every Sunday was like a family reunion. Church would be over and people wouldn't leave. They'd stay and talk long after the official ending. It was a phenomenal season of blessing and provision. As long as I live I will look back on those first years of pastoring with great fondness and a sense of what it felt like to trust God for everything.

The Cross – it's all about relationship

The Cross is *the* symbol of Christianity for obvious reasons, but also for some 'not-so-obvious' reason[s]. The obvious reason is the fact that Jesus Christ was crucified on the Roman's instrument of choice fo[r] inflicting the greatest pain and humiliation inhumanly possible.

One of the not-so-obvious reasons is the fact that the cross represents a dynamic of Christianity only understood by those for whom the cross has become their identity. That dynamic is relationship.

The cross is comprised of two beams; one vertical and one horizontal. The vertical beam represents our relationship to God. The horizontal beam represents our relationship to others in the human family.

The horizontal beam is wholly dependent upon the vertical beam to maintain it's place. Without the vertical beam it is impossible for the horizontal beam to function.

That's the way it is in the 'family' of Christianity. Our relationship with God is the basis of our relationship with each other. Only as we are in right relationship with our Father can we hope to be in right relationship with others[.]

Christianity is all about relationship; first with our Creator, and then and only then, with His creation.

Jesus, God's Son, came from the Father, not to establish a religion, but to restore a relationship; relationship that was broken by sin, which is man's disobedience to God's moral law. Through His obedience we have the opportunity to be in right relationship to our Creator, God, and in right relationship with our human family.

God, by His Spirit, lives in everyone who places their faith in Jesus, and as we submit to the work of His Spirit, He gives us the ability to love, to serve, and to give in ways that would never be possible in our own power. Although no one will ever walk through this life perfectly like Jesus, we know that His Spirit is changing us and empowering us to be like Him.

Billy Blackwood, January 2001

The Cross = Relationship

21

Divorce

I ONCE READ A QUOTE THAT CAUGHT MY EYE. It stated, "Everyone has chapters in their life they'd rather not be read aloud." I would add that I have a few I'd rather not be read at all! But, there are chapters that are an unfortunate and unpleasant part of my life that have shaped who I am and highlight my deep need of a Savior. This is one of them. My goal in sharing this chapter of my life is not to cast blame. My goal is to identify as a fallen sinner in need of a Savior. "All have sinned and fall short of the glory of God" (Rom. 3:23). There is not one of us who doesn't have something in life we would rather not be broadcast. None of us lives a perfect life. Only One Man ever did that and He did so to be a perfect sacrifice for fallen people.

After my rededication to the Lord in 1975 I was very thankful God had forgiven me and very exuberant in my expression of that forgiveness. What I didn't realize was that I had just begun the process and I was still a long way from being a healthy person. I naively assumed life would be clear sailing from there on out but failed to see the ways in which I had developed assumptions and attitudes about life that were not conducive to living out godly and healthy relationships. Looking back at those things I see more clearly the destructive patterns and self-centered immaturity that constituted my outlook on life. Far from being a godly man, I was still operating in my flesh. Oh, I read my Bible daily, went to church, and did a lot of the "right" things, but I simply failed to realize the depravity in the depths of my heart. I know scripture declares that, "If anyone is in Christ, he is a new creation; old things have passed away; behold, all things have become new." (2 Cor. 5:17). I interpreted that to mean I would no longer struggle with the "old things" and "old ways."

My wife and I met on a mission trip in 1989 and married the next year. We traveled in music ministry for a few years before I took the position at the Hendersonville Chapel. We founded GateWay Worship Center in 2001 along with members of our family and close friends. We had differences as all couples do and we sincerely worked to overcome them. However, as GateWay grew so did the chasm between my wife and me. We had some significant problems in the leadership of our church, which included family members. It wouldn't be appropriate or beneficial for me to share the details, but we experienced a church split that resulted in me becoming depressed and disillusioned. I sought comfort in a woman who was not my wife. Although our relationship was not sexual in nature it, nevertheless, wounded my wife to the core. The split in our church followed by the dissolution of our marriage was an attack of the enemy that brought it all down.

My failure as a husband and a leader in the church was obvious to everyone. In our subsequent divorce I lost my marriage, my family, my job, my income, and my reputation in the community of believers. I spent the next three years in a cave of shame and obscurity working in a machine shop. I had lost everything that meant anything to me. I struggled just to make ends meet.

As I look back over my life, I realize I have had friends from very diverse backgrounds and situations. I am particularly struck by how some of them have never been involved in anything inappropriate.

They've never been in the wrong place, they've never said the wrong thing, and they've never compromised their walk with God as far as anyone can tell. And then there are people on the other end of the spectrum who have made terrible choices and hurt and wounded loved ones along the way. The landscape of their life is marked with craters and evidence of relational explosions that have left a battlefield of casualties. And then there are people along that spectrum who may not occupy either end but fall somewhere in between, but none of us, not even those at the first end of that spectrum, have lived perfectly. We may have managed to make the right choices most of the time, but all of us have attitudes and actions that fall short of God's perfection. It is precisely because of this fact that God sent His Son, Jesus, to die in our place for our sin. 2 Corinthians 5:21 says, "He (God) made Him (Jesus) Who knew no sin to be sin for us that we might become the righteousness of God in Him." What a powerful verse! What a powerful truth!

As time has passed I have found God to be more gracious than I ever knew. I've learned that when you fall, if you'll keep taking every right step you know to take you will eventually walk out of the valley. And, of course, you also find that even though you walk through the valley of the shadow of death, death to a marriage, death to reputation, death to whatever you hold dear, you discover God was walking with you all the time and that He is a God of healing and restoration, a God of forgiveness, grace and mercy.

I also learned that when you fall you find out who your friends really are. He brought people alongside me who loved me unconditionally and helped me to put my life back together. Please excuse the somewhat unpleasant metaphor, but I've described my life during that period as being in the toilet. And when your life is in the toilet you discover there are three kinds of people. The largest group pretends they don't see you or the toilet. The next smaller group recognizes you and the toilet and walks the other way as quickly as possible. The third very select group recognizes you and the toilet and rolls up their sleeves and reaches in to help you out, ignoring the stench and the disruption to their life and schedule and does the hard work of restoring you. Bill Gabers, Gary Moore and Jim Black were three of those people in my life. I'm not sure I would have survived that season were it not for their love and dedication to my restoration. Galatians 6:1-2 says, "Brethren, if any man is overtaken in a trespass, you who are spiritual restore such a one in a spirit of gentleness, considering yourself lest you also be tempted. Bear one another's burdens and so fulfill the law of Christ."

I would love to tell you I never failed. I would love to tell you my marriage and family were restored. Neither of those is true. What I can tell you is that God knew about my failures and sin before the foundation of the world and while He doesn't excuse them, He does forgive them.

As I have opportunity to speak publicly, I often find myself saying, "It's not about how good we are; it's about how good God is!" Some people claim God isn't very gracious if He lets people go to hell. I say that the fact that He doesn't send us all there proves how gracious He is! We all deserve to pay for our sin, "But God, Who is rich in mercy, because of His great love with which He loved us, even when we were dead in trespasses, made us alive together with Christ (by grace you have been saved), and raised us up together, and made us sit together in the heavenly places in Christ Jesus, that in the ages to come He might show the exceeding riches of His grace in His kindness toward us in Christ Jesus. For by grace you have been saved through faith, and that not of yourselves; it is the gift of God, not of works, lest anyone should boast" (Ephesians 2:4-9). Praise God! Thank You, Father, for Your indescribable gift!

I have a song called "Live Today" with the lyrics, "*There's not one of us who makes it through this life without regret; things we wish we'd done; things we've done we wish we could forget. Though there's nothing we can do to change one moment of the past, tomorrow's past is what we do today. Live today, it's a gift God's given you, and there's no time like the present, give today all that God has given you. You will find your life when you give it away, live today."* Wherever you are on that spectrum, I pray that you live today!

22

Restoration

As I mentioned in the previous chapter, I spent three years working in a machine shop for barely above minimum wage. The work was grueling and dirty, burning up in the summer and freezing in the winter. As hard as it was, I look back on it with a sense of purpose. God used that time in my life to refine me. I had lost everything that meant anything to me, primarily an every day and night relationship with my kids. My employer allowed me to show up late to work every morning so I could go pick my kids up and take them to school just to have twenty minutes with them on school mornings.

I neither want to gloss over that season nor go on and on about it. It was what it was and I'm just thankful I lived through it. I learned a lot about God, finding Him to be more gracious and forgiving than I realized. I learned a lot about myself as well. When your life is reduced to the bare minimum you learn to appreciate everything. My sweet mom stood by me and prayed for me. My brother and sister-in-law did as well. There were days when I wondered if I would ever have a normal life again. I poured my time into my kids, so thankful to have their company and their love.

Little by little God began to restore quality of life to me. As I walked the path of restoration with the help of the men who reached into the toilet, I began to see a light at the end of the tunnel. Relationships began to heal. Within a year or so I was even back at the church I had pastored, helping to lead worship or playing drums for other leaders. I had no idea what the future held. I just walked each day, trusting God had a plan for my life and would reveal it to me on a need-to-know basis.

My brother, Jimmy, was leading the Blackwood Brothers Quartet, the group our dad, James, uncles Roy and Doyle, and cousin R.W., Sr. had started many years before. In 2009 the group was celebrating 75 years as a continuous musical entity. Daywind Records approached Jimmy in the summer of that year about signing the group as an artist and producing a record to coincide with the anniversary. The papers were signed and preparation began for the recording.

Dottie Leonard Miller started Daywind Records in my adopted hometown of Hendersonville, Tennessee. Many years before they signed the Blackwood Brothers to a recording contract, Dottie's son, Ed, often visited the youth group of the Chapel when I was the youth pastor there. He had been in my home on occasion when the youth group was there for functions. Ed was now a grown man and running the day-to-day operations of the company. They tapped Michael Sykes, whom I had also known for many years, to produce the record.

When Jimmy came to Hendersonville from his home in Memphis to meet with the company to begin mapping out the recording process and song selection, he stayed with me. My home was literally five minutes from Daywind. The night before the planning meeting I asked him if he would mind if I tagged along. I had seen neither Ed nor Michael in a long time and I thought it would good to see some old acquaintances. I also somewhat boldly asked

Jimmy what he would think about me playing drums on the record. I was the only drummer the Blackwood Brothers had ever had, I had played on literally hundreds of recording sessions during my years in Hendersonville/Nashville, this was a 75th Anniversary recording, and I had the right last name for the job. He thought it was a great idea and presented it to Ed and Michael who agreed.

As the planning proceeded and the songs were being selected I saw a need for arranging and offered to help arrange the vocals for the guys. Once again, I got a green light to do that and began the process of arranging the vocals for the record. In order to accomplish that task, I wrote out the charts or chord progressions for the songs to have a musical framework for the arrangements. Although I had dropped out of the recording session world when I went into full-time solo ministry in the mid-eighties, arranging was something I had done many times in both playing on others' records or producing records for artists who used my services.

The next part of the plan was the hiring of players, which was completely Michael Sykes's call, but as the Lord would have it, he hired a longtime friend, Gary Prim, to play piano. Gary had played for the Hinsons way back in the day and he and I had played on numerous recording sessions together through the years. He has been one of the most sought-after session pianists in Nashville for many years. I was excited to get to reconnect with him as well. When we met with Gary to go through the process of choosing the keys and sorting out the basic band arrangements, I mentioned to him I was helping arrange the vocals and had written charts for the songs and offered them to him if it would save him the step of having to write all of them. He was very grateful and ended up using those charts for the recording itself. I was excited about the recording session, the opportunity to be back in that environment, to be creating something that was a new chapter for the Blackwood Brothers, to be working with Michael and Gary and my brother, Jimmy. But I was completely unprepared for what happened next.

On the eve of the recording, the Blackwood Brothers were singing in St. Louis. They were leaving after that concert and heading to Nashville to record the 75th Anniversary record the next day. Out of nowhere the baritone singer and pianist for the group, Brad White, decided he didn't want to be a part of it. I think in hindsight Brad knew in his heart God was up to something with me being involved, and he was more than capable of traveling by himself and doing very well. He is a talented musician, singer, and minister and really didn't need the Blackwood Brothers Quartet. Brad had grown up as a big fan of my dad and played for several years for my dad both as an accompanist when my dad performed as a soloist and in a group my dad had called the James Blackwood Quartet in the late eighties/early nineties. That group included the great tenor, Larry Ford, Ken Turner on bass, Ray Shelton on baritone, and Brad on piano. Brad had also been instrumental, no pun intended, in keeping the Blackwood Brothers together. After my dad's group discontinued traveling, he continued to perform with Larry Ford and Ken Turner and then Wayne Little and my cousin, Mark, after the death of Cecil Blackwood, who led the Blackwood Brothers after my dad retired from it in 1981. Mark had left after my brother Jimmy rejoined the group in the early 2000s.

So, here we were in the studio ready to record and no baritone singer. I had arranged the vocals and written the charts for the record and was playing drums on it so I was intimately aware of all the moving parts and had the heart, for obvious reasons, to make this a great record. The vocals we were recording that day were not "keepers." They were strictly for reference. We were just getting the band tracks. So, when it came time to record the vocals Jimmy said, "Why don't you just sing the part?" By that time I think Jimmy, Wayne, and Randy Byrd, the bass singer for the group at the time, had seen the writing on the wall so to speak, and collectively felt this was probably God's doing.

I had, on occasion, filled in for Brad when he had a conflict between his solo schedule and the group schedule. It wasn't like I didn't have a rapport with the guys. The main concern for them and for me was I had left the group in 1973 to pursue a solo ministry, writing my own songs, which were much more on the ballad side of music, and had led worship in churches. Southern gospel was not a genre I had ever attempted to sing and anyone who knows will tell you, it is not James Taylor or Don Moen or Chris Tomlin. The style of singing is completely different than how I sang as a soloist and worship leader. But, I began to believe God was leading me to be a part of the Blackwood Brothers Quartet after a thirty-five-year hiatus.

I officially rejoined the group in November of 2009, singing baritone. It was the first time since the late 1940s that there were actually two Blackwood brothers singing together in the Blackwood Brothers! My uncles, Roy and Doyle, had retired in the late forties, which left my dad and his nephew, R.W. in the group. When R.W. was killed in the plane crash in 1954, his little brother, Cecil joined the group. In 1970 both Jimmy and I joined the group, but I was playing drums and not part of the vocal group. R.W., Jr., sang with the group for a number of years in the 1980s along with Jimmy and Cecil, but they were cousins, nephew and uncle, not brothers. Jimmy had left the group in 1986 to pursue a solo ministry and rejoined in the early 2000s at the behest of Mark, who later left the group. So, although there has always been a Blackwood at the helm, this was the first time in sixty years that two Blackwood brothers actually formed the nucleus of the quartet.

I was just thankful to be out of the machine shop!

Recording our 75th Anniversary record at Ron Fairchild's studio, Hendersonville, Tennessee, November 2009, l-r, Jimmy, Wayne Little, producer, Michael Sykes, me, Randy Byrd

During our 75th recording project, Ann Downing drops by to say hello. L-r, me, Randy Byrd, Ann Downing, Jimmy, Ron Fairchild

The BBQ on the cover of Singing News, September 2010

23

Past To Present

My brother, Jimmy, retired from the helm of the Blackwood Brothers in 2012, leaving me as the lone Blackwood in the group. And so, after my journey through the Elvis years, my time in contemporary Christian music, and ten-plus years pastoring, here I am back in the Blackwood Brothers, only this time I'm leading and managing the group. God has such a sense of humor!

One of the great blessings of having a gospel music life is the relationships that are built along the way. Because my dad was so well liked and such a great leader, I had favor with his peers by default. People like J.D. Sumner, Hovie Lister, Jake Hess, Brock and Ben Speer, George Younce and so many more were a part of my world simply because I was fortunate enough to be born into the Blackwood family. I also had a front row seat to the changes in the gospel music world that resulted from the Jesus movement of the early 1970s. The birth of contemporary Christian music out of southern California impacted the southern gospel world as groups like the Imperials found a way to bridge the gap between them. Andrae Crouch and the Disciples were building a musical bridge as well between the black gospel world and southern gospel as more and more southern gospel artists sang his great songs. It has been an exciting time to be alive and to be a part of seeing music making history.

Along with the aforementioned legends in southern gospel music, there are many people in my life's journey who have impacted me deeply in many ways. "Big" John Hall sang bass with the Blackwood Brothers in the 1960s. He and my dad were very close and to this day we keep in touch. Larry Orrell has been as dear a friend as anyone could have. They, along with Jim Black, and Charles and Barb Novell are just a few who have poured into me when I was empty and dry. There are others but let me just state that my life would be immeasurably poorer without the friends through whom God has blessed my life.

In 1998 the Blackwood Brothers were inducted into the Gospel Music Hall of Fame. In 2013 we had the honor of being inducted into the Memphis Music Hall of Fame, and in 2018 we were honored with a Brass Note in The Walk of Fame on Beale Street during our performance at the Memphis Quartet Show in June of that year. Also, in 2017 and 2018, we were invited to be a part of the first and second annual Graceland Gospel Christmas Concerts in Memphis, during which we sang before hundreds of Elvis fans. In August of 2019 we were also a part of celebrating Elvis Week with two performances at Graceland.

In addition to my concerts with the Blackwood Brothers I also have the wonderful opportunity to lead worship on occasion. One of those events is the annual conference in Phoenix called Athletes International Ministries. There are some exciting new doors opening for me to exercise my passion for leading corporate worship and helping others enjoy His presence. Whether I am leading worship with a Chris Tomlin or Hillsong chorus or singing "I'd Rather Have Jesus" or "He Touched Me," I feel God's pleasure when I sing and invite His presence to inhabit our praises. I believe this is my greatest gift and I am most at home when I have the opportunity to exercise it.

Although traveling and ministering this great music is a wonderful experience, anyone who does it for a living will tell you that being away from family at home is a big downside to being in gospel music ministry. It is the calling of God on my life that assures me I am doing what God would have me do, and often it is the testimony of people that fuels the desire to keep going, like the time in Kansas when a sweet old lady came up to our merchandise table on her walker. As she made her way toward me I wondered what was on her heart. She seemed a bit emotional. Fighting back tears she said, "My husband died six months ago and this is the first time I've been to a function and the first time I've smiled since he passed away. Thank you for blessing me today."

Not long ago we sang in Phoenix at a seniors conference. As we concluded our concert I felt led to extend an invitation for people to receive Christ. Three seniors lifted their hands and prayed to accept Christ's invitation to become a part of the family of God. It is experiences like these and many others that remind me of why I leave home and get on a bus to travel and sing. God honors His word and as we proclaim it in song the Holy Spirit speaks to the hearts of people regarding their relationship with Christ. I often tell people God didn't send Jesus to establish a religion but to restore a relationship; a relationship that is broken by sin. 2 Corinthians 5:21 says, "God made Him (Jesus), Who knew no sin to be sin for us that we become the righteousness of God in Him." Praise God! That's who we, as Christians, are!

All around us there are those who are hurting. People are so good at masking it on the outside, but God sees our hearts and uses the words of encouragement in our songs to minister to those hurts. Songs like "He Touched Me," "The Blood Will Never Lose Its Power," and "Learning To Lean" remind us how God is involved in the lives of people and wants to minister to us on a daily basis. "Beulah Land" and "What A Day That Will Be" assure us a better day awaits those of us who have placed our faith and trust in God and what Jesus did for us on the cross. As we sing the old hymns, "In the Garden," "It Is Well," and "Power In The Blood" we recall the timeless theology that is the bedrock of our faith.

Gospel Music Hall of Fame Induction Ceremony, 1998, front row, l-r, Alden Toney, Jimmy, me, James, R.W., Jr., Eric Winston, back row, l-r, Rick Price, Mike Lo Prinzi, John Hall, Chris Blackwood, Cecil

Gospel Music Hall of Fame Induction Ceremony, 1998, front row, l-r, Alden Toney, me, James, J. D. Sumner, Cecil, R.W., Jr., back row, l-r, Rick Price, John Hall, Mike LoPrinzi, Eric Winston

The BBQ and the Statler Brothers, 2012, l-r, me, Wayne Little, Jimmy, Mike Hammontree, Phil Balsley, Don Reid, Randy Byrd, Harold Reid

The BBQ performing at the Memphis Music Hall of Fame Induction Ceremony, November 2013, l-r, Wayne Little, Mike Helwig, Butch Owens, me

Memphis Music Hall of Fame Award, 2013

The BBQ & The Oak Ridge Boys at Daywind Studios, Hendersonville, Tennessee, recording "Long Gone", a song I wrote with Kenna West and Jason Cox for our "Forever" CD, 2013, l-r, William Lee Golden, Richard Sterban, Mike Helwig, Wayne Little, Joe Bonsall, me, Butch Owens, Duane Allen.

The BBQ on the cover of Singing News, November 2015, clockwise from left, Wayne Little, Butch Owens, Mike Helwig, me

Honored with a Brass Note Award for the Walk of Fame on Beale Street in Memphis, 2018, l-r, Wayne Little, Mike Helwig, Jimmy Blackwood, me, Jonathan Mattingly, and Butch Owens.

The BBQ with the Brass Note Award embedded on Beale Street, June 2019, l-r, Jonathan Mattingly, Butch Owens, Wayne Little, me.

The Brass Note Award, Beale Street, Memphis, Tennessee

The BBQ performing at Elvis Week, Graceland Sound Stage, Memphis, Tennessee, August 2019, l-r, me, Jonathan Mattingly, Butch Owens, Wayne Little

The BBQ with Elvis Radio Host, Rob Walker, Graceland, Memphis, Tennessee, August 2019, l-r, Rob Walker, Jonathan Mattingly, Wayne Little, me, Butch Owens

A bevy of Blackwoods at Elvis Week, Graceland, Memphis, Tennessee, August 2019, seated, l-r, Jimmy, Billy, Terry, standing, Jimmy's wife, Mona, my wife, Cherry, Cecil's daughter, Barbara, Terry's wife, Tina.

With friends, Don & Harold Reid of the Statler Brothers, 2015

My wife, Cherry, and I with friends, Bill & Gloria Gaither, 2016

With Pat Boone, 2017

Cherry and I with friends, Rev. Dr. Howard and Mrs. Barbara Russell, 2019

Cherry and I with friends, Don Moen and Geron Davis, 2019

With Col. Oliver North in Myrtle Beach, SC at a Jubilee Conference where we sang before he spoke, 2017

With Sandi Patty, at a Jubilee Conference, with whom we shared the stage. She shared with me that her dad was a huge Blackwood Brothers fan, 2017

Daddy and me when he and my mom surprised me at my concert at Northern Kentucky University in Highland Heights, Kentucky, circa 1988. I invited him up on stage, and when the audience asked him to sing a song he pulled a cassette accompaniment track out of his shirt pocket. The audience burst into laughter as did we. Someone took this picture to capture that moment. Daddy's nickname should have been "Everready!" but most people just called him, "Mr. Gospel Music."

Daddy on stage at Medinah Temple, Chicago, Illinois, circa 1972

Daddy at home in Memphis with his nine Grammy Awards and seven Dove Awards

Epilogue

IN CHAPTER ONE I SHARED THAT DURING THE early years of the last century part of the rural church life included an event known as, 'All Day Singing and Dinner on the Ground.' For those unfamiliar with the term, it's actually pretty self-explanatory, but let me give it some life.

In rural America in the early twentieth century, many country churches would plan an event where families would prepare meals to share with others and would bring them to church. After church services were concluded families would go outside and spread quilts and blankets on the ground under the shade trees and their families would unpack the meals they had brought. There would be ham and fried chicken and mashed potatoes, corn, beans, fresh baked bread, pies galore and at least a gallon or two of sweet tea or lemonade. As the families ate and shared their meals with others and visited with fellow church members, people would open hymnals and sing as soloists, duos, trios, or quartets, hence the name, 'All Day Singing and Dinner on the Ground.' (It was the precursor to modern day potluck suppers.)

The story is told that one morning a young couple was preparing to leave for church when they remembered that it was 'All Day Singing and Dinner on the Ground' day, and they had failed to prepare any food for themselves much less something to share. They hastily opened the cupboard and grabbed some peanut butter and jelly and bread and made a couple of PBJs and put them in a little brown paper bag.

After service concluded families began to make their way outside for the afternoon. They were spreading their quilts on the ground and spreading their meals out as well. One lady with a large family and food to feed them noticed the young couple with their brown paper bag and their peanut butter and jelly sandwiches and she called to them and said, "hey, if you would like you can join us. Just put your food in with ours and we'll all eat together!"

The young man, not being the sharpest knife in the drawer, was indignant. With a bit of an attitude he responded, "You're just trying to get our peanut butter and jelly sandwiches!"

We laugh at his insolence, but the point of the story is this: are we guilty of doing the same thing to God? God says, "you give me all you have and I'll give you all I have." And sometimes in our folly and small-mindedness we think God is trying to take what we have when in reality He is trying to give us what He has. What He has is so much more than what we have. James 1:17 says, "Every good and perfect gift come from the Father of lights." Jesus said that it is the Father's good pleasure to give us the kingdom. It's not about how good you are, it's about how good God is. God is a God of abundance. He is a God Who wants to give you good gifts. It's up to us to surrender all we have to Him.

If you want to do that now you can by praying a prayer something like this... "Father God, I believe You are a good God; a Good Father Who delights in His children. Father, I've failed and I've sinned and I don't deserve anything from You. But I believe that You will forgive me, and so I confess that I am a sinner, lost without You, in desperate need of Your grace and mercy.

Father, I thank You that Your mercy withholds from me what I do deserve and Your grace gives me what I don't deserve. Father, I turn from sin and I turn toward You. Forgive me, cleanse me, accept me based upon my faith that Your Son Jesus paid my sin debt on the cross of Calvary. I believe His blood covers my sin and I claim Him today as my Savior. Your word says that all who call on Your name will be saved. Lord, I'm calling on Your name.

Father, thank You that based upon my profession of faith in Your Son, Jesus, I am forgiven, accepted and welcomed into Your family. Thank you, Father. Fill me with Your Holy Spirit and help me to live for You. In Jesus' name I ask. Amen.

It is my prayer that, until Christ returns or I finish the race He has for me here, God will continue to display His glory and grace in my life and ministry opportunities. And I pray God will continue to reveal to you His plan and purposes for your life and that You hear His voice above all the din of noise surrounding us.

Should you have any questions about what it means to be a follower of Jesus Christ, I encourage you to check out the websites listed below. There are hundreds of resources available at these and other Christian sites to help you discover who Jesus is and why it matters that we have an intimate relationship with Him. It is my sincere hope you too will find God is the answer to life's questions. As I often say, Jesus is the most exciting Person you'll ever meet, the best Friend you'll ever have, and the only Savior you'll ever need! May God bless you as you seek Him and live for Him.

www.Biblegateway.com
www.Biblehub.com
www.Crosswalk.com

You may find more information about my life and ministry on my website, www.BillyBlackwood.com, or contact me by email: billy@BillyBlackwood.com.

Appendix One

THE BLACKWOOD BROTHERS MUSICAL FAMILY TREE

The original Blackwood Brothers Quartet consisted of three brothers: Roy, Doyle and James (my dad), and Roy's son, R.W. Roy was nineteen years older than my dad and married the year my dad was born. Two years later, in 1921, he and his wife, Susie, had a son, R.W. He was only two years younger than my dad, his Uncle James. Because of their close proximity in age, James and R.W. grew up much more like brothers than did my dad with his brothers Roy and Doyle.

Roy and Susie eventually had another son, Cecil, in 1934. Doyle and James had a double wedding ceremony in 1939 and both had sons in 1943. My dad and mom had Jimmy (James, Jr.) in July. Doyle and Lavez had Terry in October. So, the original Blackwood Brothers generation was Roy, born in 1900, his sister Lena, born in 1904, Doyle, born in 1911, and James, born in 1919.

The second generation was R.W., Cecil, Lena's two daughters, Martha and Madeline, Jimmy, Terry, Kaye (Terry's sister), and me. The third generation was R.W.'s two sons, Ron and R.W., Jr., Cecil's son, Mark, along with his sisters Regina and Barbara. My reason for sharing our family tree with you is to make the point that all the male children and many of the male grandchildren of the original three brothers ended up spending our lives in gospel music.

Ron and R.W., Jr., had the Blackwood Singers for many years. Ron still promotes gospel music, while R.W., Jr., and his wife, Donna, have had a very successful career both in Pigeon Forge, Tennessee and in Branson, Missouri with The Blackwoods Breakfast Show. Terry sang with the Stamps from 1962-1964, then with a group called the Memphians with his dad, Doyle, for three years, and then joined the Imperials in 1968 when Jake Hess left the group. He left the Imperials in 1975 to form Andrus, Blackwood & Co. with his Imperial teammate, Sherman Andrus. They continued as a duo until 1988. Terry currently performs with Terry Blackwood's Imperials.

About the Author

BILLY BLACKWOOD's career in music began when he was ten years old. He is a singer / songwriter / worship leader with deep roots in gospel music. Billy's dad, James, was an original member of the Blackwood Brothers Quartet, who have taken gospel music around the world. They were an early influence on Elvis Presley, Johnny Cash, the Statler Brothers, the Everly Brothers, Barbara Mandrell and the Mandrell Sisters, Larry Gatlin and the Gatlin Brothers, and many others.

Billy played drums with J.D. Sumner and The Stamps Quartet in his early years, as well as with the Blackwood Brothers as a teenager, making the career switch to secular music in the mid-seventies as part of Voice, an opening act with The Elvis Presley Show. He also toured for seven years as drummer with contemporary Christian musical artists Andrus, Blackwood & Co.

Billy is currently the leader/manager of the Blackwood Brothers Quartet, singing approximately 120 concerts a year in the U.S., Canada and abroad. Billy is married to his beautiful wife, Cherry, and has five children, four stepchildren, and four grandkids, with one on the way.

CPSIA information can be obtained
at www.ICGtesting.com
Printed in the USA
JSHW040509011020
8405JS00002B/2